Home Cooking

WITH AMY COLEMAN

Volume 3

Based on the Public Television Series
SPONSORED BY KITCHENAID

Home Cooking

WITH AMY COLEMAN

Volume 3

Produced by Marjorie Poore Productions

Photography by Darla Furlani

Contents

Introduction

We like to think of HOME COOKING with Amy Coleman, *now entering its third year on public television, as a different kind of cooking show. Each week* viewers meet new cookbook authors, watching their *recipes jump off the printed page and become real, edible creations. It's a weekly cooking class with some of the best experts in the country.*

We are fortunate that so many talented authors *are willing to make the long trek to Vancouver where we tape our programs every summer. While many of the authors are seduced by Vancouver's long summer days, its spectacular scenery, and its outstanding restaurants, their real motivator seems to be their genuine enthusiasm and pleasure in sharing cooking experiences and knowledge with other people. Pastry guru Rose Levy Beranbaum* (The Pie and Pastry Bible) *experimented with over 150 pie dough recipes before arriving at one worthy enough for her loyal following. Author Sam Gugino, tired of hearing "time" as the excuse for not cooking, created a book filled with meals that take only fifteen minutes to prepare* (Cooking to Beat the Clock). Saveur *magazine's editor, Colman Andrews, shared his magazine's prized fried chicken recipe, culled from travels to the backroads of the South.* New York Times *writer and entertaining expert Marian Burros* (The New Elegant but Easy Cookbook) *shared some great tips and recipes to help people put the pleasure back into entertaining. So did* Good Housekeeping's *editor, Susan Westmoreland, who recreated a meal that got everyone's seal of approval* (The Good Housekeeping Step-by-Step Cookbook). *Chris Schlesinger* (License to Grill) *came straight to Vancouver from a weeklong trip to France and pulled off*

a grilling extravaganza that left everyone swooning. The exuberant Jean-Pierre Brehier, whose "Incredible Cuisine" is just that, traveled all the way from Florida for his appearance.

For many of our guests, the contents of their suitcases *revealed what was in store. Jasper White (Lobster at Home) came to our studio with a box of feisty, but delectable, New England lobsters, which he transformed into some spectacular dishes. Marcel Desaulniers, the man who turned chocolate into a religion, (Death by Chocolate), arrived armed with boxes of cookies from his Trellis restaurant. Atlanta's Shirley Corriher (CookWise) never travels without whole nutmeg and a mini grater in her purse. She filled the studios with her gentle warmth and the unforgettable aromas of her Southern cooking. Rafael Palomino (Bistro Latino), who has made Latin cooking a rage in New York City, had a suitcase filled with authentic Colombian chorizo, Latin spices, and his breathtaking caramel Arequipe cheesecake. John Willingham (John Willingham's World Champion Bar-B-Q) drove up all the way from Memphis in a car loaded with Memphis-style barbecue sauce, special seasonings, "holy burger" utensils, pellets, and the other trappings of great barbecue. Lynne Rossetto Kasper (The Splendid Table) came with her own wheel of aged Parmesan and nearly priceless aged balsamic vinegar (we almost hired a security guard), which she used for some outrageously delicious Italian recipes. Three boxes filled with glue guns and holiday ornaments arrived just ahead of the talented Marlene Sorosky (Season's Greetings, Fast and Festive Meals for the Jewish Holidays) who shared some delicious and easy-to-make* holiday recipes. Grace Young (The Wisdom of the Chinese Kitchen) brought her parents to the studio, who are the inspiration for her wonderful collection of Chinese family recipes.

From the West Coast came Emily Luchetti (Stars' Desserts) who showed us why she and San Francisco are stars in the culinary world with a complete lesson on making tarts. Biba Caggiano (Italy al Dente), who has brought a bit of Italy to Sacramento, California, showed us the heart and soul of Italian cooking. We were blessed with a visit from the savvy Marion Cunningham (The Fannie Farmer Cookbook), who has taken on what may be the most difficult culinary topic of all: teaching people who can't cook. Southern California was represented with style and charm by Laurie Burrows Grad (Entertaining Light and Easy) who made a spectacular, guilt-free dinner. Likewise, Neelam Batra (From Chilis to Chutneys) proved that her beloved Indian cooking can also be healthy, delicious, and easy to make.

It was a bit easier for three of our guests who lived within walking distance of the studio: Denis Blais of the Monterey Lounge and Grill in the Pacific Palisades Hotel, Chris Johnson of Raincity Grill, and Robert Clark of C Restaurant. They demonstrated some wonderful recipes, showing why Vancouver is such a great restaurant city.

It is truly an exciting and talented group of culinary experts whose recipes fill this book, ready for you to try at home. I'm certain they will infuse your kitchen with as much satisfaction and fun as we had in preparing them on the programs.

—Marjorie Poore, Producer

✳ Acknowledgments

When HOME COOKING was just an idea on paper, the folks at **KitchenAid Portable Appliances** immediately saw the potential of bringing, through national television, the best culinary experts into peoples homes on a weekly basis. After all, even the best appliances need good cooking skills and great recipes to go along with them. Now, with three successful seasons on the air, KitchenAid continues to support HOME COOKING and the diverse group of talented authors it features. We owe a great deal of thanks to Brian Maynard who has supported the project in countless ways with his leadership, vision, and the overriding mission of educating consumers to be better cooks. A special thank you also goes to Ken Kaminski and the many others at KitchenAid who have supported HOME COOKING.

Hats off also to our exuberant and talented host, Amy Coleman, who has graciously welcomed guests into the HOME COOKING studio kitchen, making them feel at home, and working with them side by side to prepare all those wonderful dishes. Her hard work, dedication, and knowledge continue to shine through at all times and make the programs fun and interesting to watch.

There are numerous companies who have provided invaluable support to the project: Thank you to the Weber-Stephen Products Co. for their extraordinary grills; Colavita for their outstanding olive oil and other Italian food products; Pacific Palisades hotel and apartments in Vancouver for providing us with such sumptuous and comfortable accommodations; The Meyer corporation for providing us with their excellent line of Anolon pots and pans. A special thank you to Villeroy & Boch for their exquisite dishes with so many luscious colors and striking patterns; Vietri, another company which makes our food look good with their gorgeous Italian plates and dishes; Norpro who has kept our kitchen well-stocked with every tool and gadget imaginable; Mango Imports for their beautiful kitchen textiles; Emile Henry for their wonderful, colorful and diverse cookware and tableware; Callebaut for baking chocolate worthy of its outstanding reputation; and Le Creuset for their hard-working and colorful cookware.

—Marjorie Poore and Alec Fatalevich

STARTERS, SOUP AND SALADS

Crab-Stuffed Mushrooms

MARLENE SOROSKY / REPRINTED FROM *SEASON'S GREETINGS* **(CHRONICLE BOOKS)**

18 medium-size mushrooms
(about 1 pound)
7 ounces crabmeat, cartilage removed
(*see note*)
5 scallions with tops, finely chopped
1/4 teaspoon dried thyme, crumbled
1/4 teaspoon dried oregano, crumbled
1/4 teaspoon dried savory, crumbled
Freshly ground black pepper to taste
1/4 cup finely grated Parmesan cheese
1/3 cup regular or low-fat mayonnaise
Grated Parmesan cheese, for topping
Paprika, for topping

✳ Preheat the oven to 350°F. Wipe the mushrooms clean with a damp towel. Remove the stems and discard them. Scrape out the gills and any remaining stems with a spoon, making deep cups.

✳ Stir the crabmeat, scallions, thyme, oregano, savory, and pepper together in a small bowl. Stir in 1/4 cup Parmesan cheese and the mayonnaise, mixing with a fork until combined. Fill the mushroom caps with rounded teaspoonfuls of the filling, and place them in an ungreased shallow baking dish. Bake for 15 minutes.

✳ The filled mushrooms may be covered and refrigerated overnight. Reheat them at 350°F for 7 to 10 minutes, or until hot.

✳ Sprinkle the tops with additional Parmesan cheese and paprika. Place the mushrooms under the broiler for 2 minutes, or until lightly browned.

NOTE: The filling can be made with fresh or canned crabmeat. If using canned, be sure to rinse it first.

SERVES 9

THERE IS AN ONGOING debate ABOUT THE PROPER WAY TO clean MUSHROOMS. MARLENE MAKES IT easy: JUST WIPE THEM WITH A DAMP TOWEL TO preserve THEIR TEXTURE. THESE cheesy NIBBLES CAN BE ASSEMBLED AHEAD OF time, REFRIGERATED OVERNIGHT, AND HEATED JUST AS THE guests ARE ARRIVING.

Toasted Mushroom Rolls

MARIAN BURROS / REPRINTED FROM *THE NEW ELEGANT BUT EASY COOKBOOK* (SIMON & SCHUSTER)

MAKES 42 ROLLS

IF YOU CAN FIND wild MUSHROOMS, THEY WILL LEND A deep EARTHY FLAVOR TO THESE CIGAR-SHAPED APPETIZERS. PICK THE SOFT, spongy TYPE OF WHITE SANDWICH BREAD TO roll AROUND THE MUSHROOM FILLING, JELLY ROLL-STYLE.

½ pound white mushrooms or exotic mushrooms like portobello, cremini, shiitake, or some combination

4 tablespoons (½ stick) unsalted butter, plus melted butter for brushing

3 tablespoons flour

1 cup light cream or half-and-half

1 tablespoon minced fresh chives

1 teaspoon lemon juice

Salt and freshly ground pepper to taste

21 slices white bread (two 16-ounce loaves), crusts removed

✳ Wash, trim, dry, and finely chop the mushrooms. Sauté them in 4 tablespoons hot butter for about 3 or 4 minutes. Remove from the heat and blend in the flour. Stir in the cream and return to the heat, cooking until the mixture thickens. Remove from the heat. Stir in the chives and lemon juice. Season with salt and pepper. Let cool.

✳ With a rolling pin, roll the bread slices thin. Spread each slice with some of the mushroom mixture; roll up and place, seam side down, on cookie sheets. Brush with additional melted butter. Leave on the cookie sheets and freeze, if desired, or refrigerate. After the rolls are frozen or chilled, they can be removed from the sheets and stored in a plastic bag, if desired.

✳ To serve, let the frozen rolls defrost; preheat the oven to 400°F. Toast on all sides for about 15 minutes, until the rolls are golden. Cut in half and serve warm, not hot.

Zucchini Sausage Squares

MARLENE SOROSKY / REPRINTED FROM *SEASON'S GREETINGS* (CHRONICLE BOOKS)

MAKES 40 SQUARES

MAKE THIS no-frills
APPETIZER WHEN UNEX-
PECTED guests APPEAR.
OR, MAKE THE SQUARES
ahead OF TIME, STORE
THEM IN THE FREEZER, AND
REHEAT THEM AS NEEDED.

1 pound (about 2 large) zucchini
12 ounces bulk pork or turkey sausage
1/2 cup chopped onion
4 large eggs
1/2 cup grated Parmesan cheese
18 Ritz crackers, crushed
  (about 1/2 cup crumbs)

1 teaspoon dried basil, crumbled
1/2 teaspoon dried oregano, crumbled
1/8 teaspoon black pepper
1 clove garlic, finely minced
1 cup (about 4 ounces) shredded sharp
  regular or low-fat cheddar cheese

✳ Preheat the oven to 325°F. Wash the zucchini, trim off the stems, and shred the zucchini; set it aside. Sauté the sausage and onion in a medium skillet, stirring to break up the
sausage, until all pink is gone; drain off all fat.

✳ Whisk the eggs in a large mixing bowl until frothy. Stir in the Parmesan cheese, cracker
crumbs, basil, oregano, pepper, garlic, sausage mixture, and zucchini. Spoon the mixture
into a greased 7 x 11-inch shallow glass baking dish, spreading the top smooth. Bake for
25 minutes. Sprinkle the top with cheddar cheese and bake 15 minutes longer. Remove
the dish from the oven, cool slightly, and cut into 1 1/2-inch squares.

✳ The squares may be covered and refrigerated overnight, or frozen. Defrost them at
room temperature. Reheat the thawed squares on a baking sheet at 350°F for 10 minutes,
or until heated through.

VARIATION: For a leaner version, substitute 2 whole eggs and 4 egg whites for the 4 eggs.
Reduce the Parmesan cheese to 1/3 cup.

Best-Ever Marinated Shrimp

SHIRLEY CORRIHER / REPRINTED FROM *COOKWISE* **(WILLIAM MORROW AND COMPANY)**

1¹/₂ pounds shrimp, cooked and peeled
1 large onion, thinly sliced
7 bay leaves
1 cup good-quality olive oil
2 tablespoons white vinegar
2 tablespoons capers, drained

2 tablespoons caper juice
2 teaspoons Worcestershire sauce,
    preferably Lea & Perrins
1 teaspoon salt
4 dashes hot pepper sauce

✳ In a large mixing bowl, alternate layers of shrimp, onion, and bay leaves. In a small bowl, whisk together the remaining ingredients. Pour over the shrimp, cover, and refrigerate overnight. Drain the vinaigrette, remove some of the onions (for aesthetics), and serve cold.

SERVES 8 TO 10

CAPERS ADD A MEDITERRA-
NEAN twist TO THIS
APPETIZER. THE SLIGHTLY
ACIDIC marinade
TENDERIZES THE SHRIMP
WITHOUT CAUSING THEM
TO FALL APART.

Sun-Dried Tomato and Basil Chicken Paté

LAURIE BURROWS GRAD / REPRINTED FROM *ENTERTAINING LIGHT AND EASY* (SIMON & SCHUSTER)

SERVES 8 TO 10

THIS PARTY DISH HAS TWO LAYERS: A LEAN paté, MADE WITH CHICKEN BREASTS AND EGG WHITES, AND A full-flavored "FROSTING" MADE OF pureed SUN-DRIED TOMATOES. FRESH BASIL, GARLIC, PARMESAN CHEESE, AND PINE NUTS GIVE IT AN ITALIAN flair.

THE PATÉ BASE AND TOPPING CAN BE PREPARED 2 TO 3 days IN ADVANCE AND HELD SEPARATELY IN THE REFRIGERATOR UNTIL ready TO SERVE.

Paté

3/4 pound boneless, skinless chicken breasts, cut into 1-inch pieces
2 egg whites
1 egg
2 medium cloves garlic, coarsely chopped
2 shallots, coarsely chopped
2 tablespoons pine nuts
One 2 1/2- to 3-ounce package sun-dried tomatoes, soaked in boiling water to cover and squeezed dry
3 tablespoons coarsely chopped fresh basil
3 tablespoons freshly grated Parmesan cheese
2 tablespoons extra-virgin olive oil
Salt and freshly ground pepper to taste

Topping

One 2 1/2- to 3-ounce package sun-dried tomatoes, soaked in boiling water to cover and squeezed dry
2 tablespoons coarsely chopped fresh basil
2 tablespoons defatted chicken broth
1 tablespoon pine nuts
1 tablespoon freshly grated Parmesan cheese
1 clove garlic, roughly chopped
Salt and freshly ground pepper to taste

Fresh basil leaves, for garnish
Pine nuts, for garnish
Lemon wedges, for garnish
Thinly sliced toast or crackers

✱ Preheat the oven to 325°F. Lightly coat the inside of a small loaf pan (about 7½ x 3½ x 2 inches) with olive oil nonstick cooking spray.

✱ In a food processor or blender, process the chicken with the remaining paté ingredients, pulsing on and off until well combined and smooth. Place the mixture in the prepared pan, seal tightly with aluminum foil, and place the loaf pan in a larger pan filled with an inch of hot water. Bake for 70 minutes, or until an inserted knife comes out clean.

✱ Remove the pan from the oven and cool on a rack for 15 to 20 minutes. Loosen the sides with a sharp paring knife, turn out on a small platter with bottom side up, and blot dry lightly with paper towels. Cover with plastic wrap, and chill for 4 to 6 hours, or overnight.

✱ Place the topping ingredients in a food processor or blender and process until smooth.

✱ Frost the paté with the sun-dried tomato-basil mixture. Serve the paté chilled or at room temperature, garnished with basil leaves, pine nuts, and lemon wedges and accompanied by thinly sliced toast or crackers.

VARIATION: Walnuts can be substituted for the pine nuts.

Spicy Chicken Little Drumsticks

SUZANNE GOODING / REPRINTED FROM *THE MAGIC SPOON COOKBOOK* **(KLUTZ PRESS)**

$^1/_4$ cup ketchup

$^1/_4$ cup barbecue sauce

Juice of 1 lemon

12 chicken drumettes

✱ Preheat the oven to 350°F. Mix the ketchup, barbecue sauce, and lemon juice in a bowl with a large spoon. Add the chicken drumettes and stir to coat evenly with sauce.

✱ Spread out on a baking sheet covered with aluminum foil and bake for 30 minutes.

✱ Use oven mitts when taking the chicken out of the oven. Use tongs to put the chicken on a platter. Serve warm.

Designer Pretzels

SUZANNE GOODING / REPRINTED FROM *THE MAGIC SPOON COOKBOOK* (KLUTZ PRESS)

1¹/₂ cups warm water	**Topping**
1 package dry yeast	2 tablespoons water
1 tablespoon sugar	1 egg
4¹/₂ cups flour	Coarse salt, poppy or sesame seeds

✸ Put the 1½ cups of warm water, yeast, and sugar in a large bowl. Let it sit for 5 minutes.

✸ Stir in the flour and mix well, first with a wooden spoon, then with your hands.

✸ Put extra flour on the counter, turn out the dough, and knead about 20 times by folding the dough over onto itself. You can bang it, slam it, or give it a good karate chop.

✸ Put the dough back in the bowl, cover with a towel, and let it rise in a warm place for about 1 hour until doubled in size.

✸ Divide the dough into 20 to 30 balls, about the size of golf balls. Use extra flour on your hands if the dough is sticky. Roll out each ball with your hands into a long stick as thick as your thumb.

✸ Shape the sticks into hearts, stars, snails, fish, pretzels, initials—anything!

✸ Turn the oven on to 400°F. Place all your creations on cookie sheets.

✸ Use a fork to mix the water and egg together in a bowl and brush on the pretzel shapes with a pastry brush. Sprinkle with coarse salt, poppy or sesame seeds or leave plain.

✸ Bake for about 20 to 25 minutes until hard and brown. Cool on a rack.

✸ If you want more bread-like pretzels, bake them for only 15 minutes (but they won't keep as well).

MAKES 20 TO 30

KIDS CAN twist THE PRETZEL DOUGH INTO THEIR FAVORITE animal FIGURES OR SHAPES. BAKE THEM LESS FOR soft, chewy PRETZELS, MORE FOR PRETZELS THAT SNAP.

Twice-Baked Brie and Roasted Pepper Soufflés with Olive Tapenade

DENIS BLAIS / EXECUTIVE CHEF, PACIFIC PALISADES HOTEL, VANCOUVER, BRITISH COLUMBIA

SERVES 8

THERE'S A surprise

WAITING FOR YOU WHEN

YOU DIG INTO THIS LIGHT

SOUFFLÉ. A STRETCH OF

WARM BRIE cheese

WILL OOZE ITS WAY ONTO

YOUR fork.

Butter to brush ramekins
1 cup fine bread crumbs
2 tablespoons butter
1/4 cup all-purpose flour
1 cup milk
3 tablespoons grated Parmesan cheese
1 large red bell pepper, roasted, peeled, seeded, and chopped
1/4 teaspoon salt
1/4 teaspoon coarsely ground black pepper
2 egg yolks

8 egg whites, whipped until soft peaks form
8 ounces Brie cheese, cut into 8 pieces

Olive Tapenade
2 medium-size red bell peppers, roasted, peeled, and seeded
2 anchovy fillets
3 cloves garlic
1/4 cup olive oil
1 cup pitted kalamata olives
Juice of 1 lemon

Mixed baby greens

✻ Preheat the oven to 375°F. Brush eight 4-ounce ramekins with butter and line with bread crumbs. Set aside.

✻ In a heavy-bottomed saucepan, stir the 2 tablespoons butter with the flour to make a roux. Stir constantly over low heat for 3 to 4 minutes. Slowly add the milk, stirring until the mixture is smooth and thick. Cook, stirring, for another 5 to 6 minutes. Remove from heat and transfer to a large bowl.

✻ Stir in the grated Parmesan, chopped red pepper, salt, and pepper.

✻ One at a time, add the egg yolks and beat until smooth. Carefully fold the beaten egg whites into the soufflé mixture.

✻ Place a piece of Brie in each prepared ramekin. Spoon in the soufflé mixture to fill the ramekins.

✻ Place the filled ramekins in a baking pan and pour enough water in the pan to come 1 inch up the sides of the ramekins. Bake for 15 minutes at 375°F.

✻ Reduce the oven heat to 300°F and bake for an additional 25 minutes, until an inserted toothpick comes out clean (be careful not to insert the toothpick into the Brie). Let cool completely.

✻ To make the tapenade, puree all of the ingredients in a food processor until smooth.

✻ To serve, carefully remove the cooled soufflés from the ramekins. Reheat the soufflés at 325°F for 10 minutes. Arrange a bed of mixed greens on each of 8 serving plates and top with a heated soufflé. Drizzle the tapenade around each soufflé and serve immediately.

Chili Salmon Spring Rolls with Oyster Sauce

CHRIS JOHNSON / EXECUTIVE CHEF, RAINCITY GRILL, VANCOUVER, BRITISH COLUMBIA

1 1/4 pounds smoked salmon,
  skin removed, cut into 1/4-inch dice

1 1/2 teaspoons ground chili paste or
  chili flakes

2 tablespoons chopped fresh cilantro

3/4 cup fresh bean sprouts

1 cup chopped fresh spinach

1 teaspoon minced fresh ginger

1/4 cup sweet soy sauce

Twelve 6 x 6-inch spring roll wrappers

Egg whites for sealing

Vegetable oil for deep frying

Fresh or pickled radishes, cut into
  thin slices, for garnish

Chopped green onions or cilantro leaves,
  for garnish

Purchased oyster sauce or plum sauce

✳ In a large mixing bowl, combine the diced salmon, chili paste or flakes, cilantro, bean sprouts, spinach, ginger, and soy sauce. Mix well, making sure all ingredients are combined thoroughly and the mixture is moist. Set aside.

✳ Lay one spring roll wrapper on a work surface with a point facing up and stretch the edges slightly to remove wrinkles. Spoon 1/12 of the salmon filling on the upper third of the wrapper, evenly distributing it. Fold over the top point and both sides of the spring roll wrapper. Starting from the top edge, roll the spring roll into a cylinder, pressing down slightly to keep the roll firm. Brush the edges with beaten egg whites to seal. Repeat the filling and rolling process with the remaining salmon mixture and spring roll wrappers.

✳ Pour about 1 inch of vegetable oil into a deep, medium-size skillet. Heat the oil until it reaches 375°F.

✳ Fry the spring rolls in the hot oil, 1 to 2 minutes, turning with tongs until each side is crisp and golden.

✳ To serve, arrange two rolls on each appetizer plate and garnish with radish slices and green onions. Serve with oyster sauce on the side for dipping.

SERVES 6

YOU'LL love THE INTERESTING MIXTURE OF flavors IN THESE CRISPY APPETIZERS. SWEET SOY sauce IS THICKER AND SWEETER THAN REGULAR soy SAUCE. YOU MAY NEED TO shop IN AN ASIAN MARKET TO FIND IT. KEEP EXTRA SPRING ROLL wrappers ON HAND, IN CASE YOU TEAR SOME.

Grilled Regular Mushrooms with Sherry

CHRIS SCHLESINGER / REPRINTED FROM *LICENSE TO GRILL* (WILLIAM MORROW AND COMPANY)

2 pounds medium mushrooms, stemmed
   and cleaned
1/4 cup olive oil
Salt and freshly cracked black pepper
   to taste

3 tablespoons unsalted butter, cut into
   small pieces
1 tablespoon minced garlic
1/2 cup roughly chopped fresh parsley
1/4 cup sherry

✳ In a medium bowl, combine the mushrooms, olive oil, and salt and pepper to taste and toss well.

✳ Grill the mushrooms over a hot fire until they are brown and soft, 3 to 5 minutes. To check for doneness: Cut into a mushroom and see if it looks moist all the way through.

✳ Remove the mushrooms from the fire and place in a medium bowl. Add the butter, garlic, parsley, and sherry and mix gently until the butter melts. Season to taste with salt and pepper and serve.

SERVES 4

DRESS smoky GRILLED MUSHROOMS WITH SHERRY, BUTTER, AND GARLIC AND SERVE THEM TO hungry GUESTS WHILE DINNER IS BEING PREPARED. PROVIDE hunks OF COUNTRY-STYLE bread TO SOAK UP UP ANY REMAINING JUICES.

Mini Corn Muffins with Chilies and Cheese

MARLENE SOROSKY / REPRINTED FROM *SEASON'S GREETINGS* (CHRONICLE BOOKS)

Creamed-Corn Muffins
$1/4$ pound (1 stick) butter or margarine
$1/2$ cup whole or low-fat milk
1 large egg, at room temperature
One $8^{1}/_{2}$-ounce can creamed corn, undrained
1 cup all-purpose flour
1 cup yellow cornmeal
1 tablespoon sugar
1 tablespoon baking powder
1 teaspoon salt
2 or 3 dashes of Tabasco sauce

Filling
One 7-ounce can diced green chilies, drained
One 2-ounce jar chopped pimientos, drained
$1^{1}/_{2}$ cups (about 6 ounces) shredded sharp cheddar cheese
1 teaspoon chili powder

✳ To make the creamed-corn muffins, preheat the oven to 425°F. Grease or spray thirty-six $1^{1}/_{2}$-inch miniature muffin cups. In a large microwave-safe bowl or saucepan, melt the butter. Cool slightly, then whisk in the milk. Whisk in the egg and the corn. Stir in the flour, cornmeal, sugar, baking powder, salt, and Tabasco; the batter will be lumpy. Spoon the batter into the muffin cups, filling them almost to the top. Bake for 15 to 20 minutes, or until the tops are golden and a cake tester inserted in the center comes out clean. Immediately remove the muffins from the tins and cool to room temperature.

✳ To make the filling, stir the chilies, pimientos, cheese, and chili powder together in a bowl.

✳ Using a small, sharp knife, cut around the tops of the muffins about $1/4$ inch from their rims. Cut down toward the bottoms of the muffins and remove some of the bread; discard the tops. Spoon the filling into the muffins, mounding the tops.

✳ The filled muffins may be covered and refrigerated overnight, or frozen. Defrost them at room temperature.

✳ Before serving, preheat the oven to 400°F. Place the muffins on baking sheets and bake for 5 minutes, or until the cheese is melted.

VARIATION: Stir the filling ingredients into the muffin batter and bake as directed. This will make about 55 mini muffins.

MAKES 36 MINI MUFFINS

CREAMED-corn MUFFINS ARE SCOOPED OUT, THEN STUFFED WITH A MIXTURE OF SHARP CHEDDAR CHEESE AND RED AND GREEN CHILE PEPPERS. IT'S AN ORIGINAL appetizer FOR YOUR CHRISTMAS PARTY BUFFET.

Curried Apple and Onion Soup

MARCEL DESAULNIERS / REPRINTED FROM *THE TRELLIS COOKBOOK* (FIRESIDE)

5 tablespoons unsalted butter
1 large onion, thinly sliced
Salt and pepper to season
5½ cups chicken stock
½ cup dry white wine
1 tablespoon vegetable oil
1 tablespoon water
1 large onion, chopped
8 stalks celery, chopped
2 medium leeks, white part only, chopped

1 tablespoon chopped fresh thyme,
   or 1 teaspoon dried
2 small bay leaves
1 tablespoon curry powder
6 tablespoons all-purpose flour
4 cups water
1 tablespoon fresh lemon juice
4 tart green apples
1 cup heavy cream

SERVES 8

GRANNY SMITH apples ARE A perfect CHOICE FOR THIS VELVETY SOUP. OR, EXPERIMENT WITH ANY VARIETY OF tart APPLES TO LEND A NEW FLAVOR.

✳ Melt 1 tablespoon of the butter in a nonstick sauté pan over medium heat. Add the sliced onion, season with salt and pepper, and sauté until the onion is golden brown, 25 to 30 minutes. Add 2½ cups of the chicken stock and the wine. Bring to a boil. Lower the heat and simmer very slowly for 15 minutes.

✳ Heat the vegetable oil and water in a 5-quart saucepan over medium heat. When hot, add the chopped onion, celery, and leeks. Season with salt and pepper and sauté for 5 minutes. Add the remaining 3 cups chicken stock. Tie the thyme and bay leaves in a small piece of cheesecloth and add to the stock and vegetables. Bring to a boil, lower the heat, and simmer for 25 to 30 minutes.

✳ Melt the remaining 4 tablespoons butter in a 2½-quart saucepan over low heat. Add the curry powder and whisk to blend. Add the flour to make a roux, and cook until the roux bubbles, 6 to 8 minutes. Stir constantly to prevent browning and scorching. Strain 2 cups of the simmering stock from the 5-quart saucepan into the roux. Whisk vigorously until smooth, then add to the remaining stock and chopped vegetables. Whisk until well combined. Bring to a boil, then reduce the heat and allow to simmer for 10 minutes.

✳ Remove the soup from the heat. Remove and discard the tied herbs. Purée the soup in a food processor fitted with a metal blade. Strain. Return to low heat in a 5-quart saucepan. Add the sliced onion and stock mixture. Hold at a simmer.

✳ Place the water and lemon juice in a large bowl. Peel, core, quarter, and slice the apples widthwise. Place the apples in the lemon-water as sliced, to prevent discoloration.

✳ Heat the cream in a nonstick sauté pan over medium heat. Drain the sliced apples in a colander. Rinse under cold running water and shake dry. When the cream is warm, add the apples and heat until the apples are hot, 3 to 4 minutes (do not boil). Add to the soup, adjust the seasoning with salt and pepper, and serve immediately.

Butternut Squash and Bourbon Bisque

JEAN PIERRE BREHIER / REPRINTED FROM *INCREDIBLE CUISINE* (TIME LIFE)

SERVES 6

THIS SATISFYING WINTER

soup IS HIGH IN FLAVOR,

BUT LOW IN FAT. PUREED

BUTTERNUT squash IS

"SOUPED UP" WITH MAPLE

SYRUP, SOY SAUCE, GINGER,

AND A dash OF BOURBON.

1 or 2 butternut squash
  (about 4 pounds total)
1 tablespoon extra-virgin olive oil
1 cup diced onion
1 cup diced leek
1/2 teaspoon ground cumin
2 tablespoons chopped fresh garlic
1 tablespoon chopped fresh ginger
2 tablespoons pure maple syrup
2 tablespoons soy sauce

1/4 cup bourbon
1/2 cup dry sherry
1/4 teaspoon freshly grated nutmeg
5 cups rich chicken stock
3/4 cup evaporated skim milk
Salt and freshly ground black pepper
  to taste
2 tablespoons cornstarch mixed with
  2 tablespoons water

✱ Preheat the oven to 375°F.

✱ With a sharp knife, prick the squash in several places to allow steam to escape while it cooks (otherwise, it could burst). Place the squash in a baking dish lined with foil and roast for about 90 minutes, until the squash is soft when you push on it. Let cool for 30 minutes, so it's easy to handle, then peel, seed, and remove the strings. Cut the roasted squash meat into 1/2-inch pieces, or scoop the meat out with a spoon.

✱ In a heavy soup kettle, heat the olive oil and add the onion. Cook until light golden brown and add the leek and cumin. Cook for 2 minutes and add the garlic and ginger. When the garlic is fragrant, add the maple syrup, soy sauce, bourbon, sherry, and nutmeg. Add the squash meat and stock and bring to a boil. Lower the heat and cook gently for 15 minutes.

✱ Using an immersion blender (or a regular blender), puree the soup until very smooth. Add the evaporated milk, salt, and pepper. Cook for 2 minutes; do not bring to a boil. Add the cornstarch mixture and serve in soup plates.

Grilled Apple and Bread Salad
with Arugula, Blue Cheese, and Grapes

CHRIS SCHLESINGER / REPRINTED FROM *LICENSE TO GRILL* (WILLIAM MORROW AND COMPANY)

2 Granny Smith apples, halved and cored

2 to 3 slices good crusty bread

1 bunch arugula, trimmed, washed, and
    torn into large pieces

2 cups seedless red grapes, halved
    (or substitute seedless green grapes)

$^1/_2$ cup olive oil

$^1/_4$ cup red wine vinegar

Salt and freshly ground black pepper
    to taste

$^1/_2$ cup crumbled blue cheese

✴ Place the apples cut side down on the grill over a medium-hot fire and cook for about 5 to 7 minutes, or until browned. At the same time, place the bread around the edge of the fire, where the heat is low, and toast for about 5 minutes, or until golden brown. Remove the apples and bread from the grill as they are done.

✴ When cool enough to handle, cut the bread into large chunks and place them in a large bowl. Cut the apples into thin slices and toss them in with the bread.

✴ Add the arugula, grapes, olive oil, vinegar, and salt and pepper to taste and toss well. Just before serving, sprinkle with the blue cheese.

SERVES 4

THIS SALAD IS A BALANC-
ING ACT OF flavors.
Tart GRANNY SMITH
APPLES LEND ACIDITY TO
THE creamy BLUE
CHEESE, AND spicy
ARUGULA IS OFFSET BY
sweet GRAPES.

Pasta and Bean Soup Neapolitan Style

BIBA CAGGIANO / REPRINTED FROM *ITALY AL DENTE* (WILLIAM MORROW AND COMPANY)

SERVES 8

A specialty FOOD STORE IS BOUND TO HAVE SALTY imported PROSCIUTTO HAM. SPLURGE ON IT — IT WILL ADD UN-MATCHED flavor TO YOUR SOUP.

IF YOU PREFER TO eat THE soup AT ROOM TEMPERATURE, LIKE MOST ITALIANS DO IN SUMMER, LEAVE THE SOUP OUT FOR SEVERAL HOURS. COOK THE pasta SEPARATELY IN SALTED BOILING WATER, DRAIN IT, AND ADD IT TO THE SOUP JUST BEFORE serving.

2 cups (1 pound) dried cranberry beans or red kidney beans, soaked overnight in cold water to cover generously

2 quarts water

1 thick slice prosciutto (2 to 3 ounces), cut into 3 or 4 pieces

1/3 cup extra-virgin olive oil

1 cup finely minced yellow onion

2 tablespoons chopped fresh parsley

3 cloves garlic, minced

1 pound ripe plum tomatoes, halved, seeded, and finely minced

Chopped fresh red chili pepper or hot red pepper flakes to taste

Salt to taste

6 ounces spaghetti, broken into small pieces

Extra-virgin olive oil to taste

✳ Drain and rinse the beans under cold running water. Put them in a large pot and add the water and the prosciutto. Cover the pot partially and bring the water to a gentle simmer. Simmer the beans over low heat, stirring occasionally, until they are tender, 45 minutes to 1 hour. Turn the heat off and set aside until ready to use.

✳ With a slotted spoon, scoop up the pieces of prosciutto from the beans and cut them into small pieces. Heat the oil in a medium saucepan over medium heat. Add the onion, parsley, and garlic. Cook, stirring, until the onion is pale yellow and soft, about 5 minutes. Add the tomatoes, prosciutto pieces and the hot pepper, then season with salt. Simmer, uncovered, until the tomatoes are soft, 10 to 12 minutes. If the tomatoes are not very ripe, and the mixture looks dry, add a few tablespoons of the bean cooking water.

✳ Puree half of the beans in a food processor or food mill and return them to the pot with the rest of the beans. Add the tomato mixture to the beans and put the pot back on medium heat. Simmer the soup 4 to 5 minutes longer. Add the spaghetti and cook, stirring occasionally, until it is tender but still firm to the bite, *al dente*. Turn the heat off under the pot and let the soup rest for a few minutes. Serve hot or at room temperature with a dash of fragrant olive oil on each serving.

On video

Tandoori Chicken Salad with Ginger-Mint Dressing

NEELAM BATRA / REPRINTED FROM *CHILIS TO CHUTNEYS: AMERICAN HOME COOKING WITH THE FLAVORS OF INDIA* **(WILLIAM MORROW AND COMPANY)**

6 cups firmly packed mixed baby greens

1 small red bell pepper, seeded and cut into 1-inch-long julienne strips

1 small yellow bell pepper, seeded and cut into 1-inch-long julienne strips

1 cup grated and squeezed pickling or Japanese cucumber *(shredded & Cuisinart)*

1/2 cup thinly sliced scallion whites, or more to taste

1 cup peeled and grated carrots *shredded & Cuisinart*

3 cups shredded or diced Chicken Tandoori *(see page 68)*, or more to taste

1/4 cup blanched almond slivers, toasted *(see note)*

1 cup Ginger-Mint Dressing *(see below)*

2 teaspoons sesame seeds, toasted *(see note)*

Freshly ground black pepper to taste

Squeeze the shredded Carrots & cucumbers after shredding in the food processor to remove excess liquid.

✳ Wash and dry the greens in a salad spinner or on a kitchen towel, then tear the larger leaves into bite-size pieces. Place them in a salad bowl and add the bell peppers, cucumber, scallion whites, and carrots. Cover and refrigerate until needed.

✳ When ready to serve, mix in the chicken and almond slivers. Add dressing to taste and toss to mix the salad. Top with the sesame seeds and pepper, and serve with additional dressing on the side.

NOTE: To pan-toast nuts, seeds, or ground spices, place them in a small nonstick skillet and cook, stirring, over moderate heat until highly fragrant and golden, 2 to 4 minutes, depending on the quantity. Transfer immediately to a bowl or plate to stop further toasting from the heat in the skillet. Cool and store in airtight containers in the refrigerator for 2 to 3 months.

1 qt. Boil milk Cool to 115-118° Spoon!

Ginger-Mint Dressing

One 1-inch piece fresh ginger, peeled and cut into thin slices

1 clove garlic, peeled

1/3 cup firmly packed fresh mint leaves

2 tablespoons fresh lime or lemon juice

1 tablespoon honey

3/4 cup nonfat plain yogurt

1/2 teaspoon salt, or to taste

✳ In the work bowl of a food processor fitted with the metal blade and the motor running, process the ginger and garlic until minced by dropping them through the feed tube. Stop the motor, add the remaining ingredients, and process again until smooth. Stop the motor and scrape down the sides of the work bowl once or twice. Remove to a bowl and refrigerate until needed. The dressing stays fresh for 8 to 10 days in the refrigerator. *Makes about 1 cup*

Traditional Lobster Salad

JASPER WHITE / REPRINTED FROM *LOBSTER AT HOME* **(SIMON & SCHUSTER)**

1 pound fully cooked lobster meat, or
    5 pounds live lobsters
1 medium cucumber (5 to 6 ounces),
    peeled, seeded, and finely diced
1/2 cup mayonnaise

3 small scallions (white and most of
    the green parts), thinly sliced
Kosher or sea salt to taste
Freshly ground black pepper to taste

✳ If using live lobsters, steam or boil them. Let them cool at room temperature. Use a cleaver to crack and remove the meat from the claws, knuckles, and tails. Remove the cartilage from the claws and the intestine from the tails of the cooked meat. Cut the meat into 1/2-inch dice. You may pick all the meat from the carcass and add it to the meat or freeze the carcass for soup or broth.

✳ Place the cucumber in a colander for at least 5 minutes to drain the excess liquid.

✳ In a bowl, combine the lobster, cucumber, and mayonnaise. If the salad is to be served within the hour, add the scallions. If not, add them 30 minutes before serving. Season with salt, if needed, and pepper. Cover with plastic wrap and chill for at least 30 minutes before serving.

SERVES 6

OFFER THIS SUMPTUOUS lobster SALAD IN A FESTIVE SERVING BOWL AT A family-style BUFFET, OR SAVE THE LOBSTER SHELLS TO SERVE INDIVIDUAL portions. YOU CAN ALSO PACK IT INTO AVOCADO OR PAPAYA HALVES, OR HOLLOWED-OUT summer SQUASH, sweet PEPPER, OR TOMATO SHELLS.

The World-Famous Maine Lobster Roll

JASPER WHITE / REPRINTED FROM *LOBSTER AT HOME* **(SIMON & SCHUSTER)**

1 recipe Traditional Lobster Salad (*see above*)
6 New England-style hot dog buns

6 tablespoons unsalted butter, softened
Pickles and potato chips for accompaniments

✳ Prepare the lobster salad and chill for at least 30 minutes.

✳ Preheat a large heavy skillet (12 or 14 inches) over medium-low heat. (A black cast-iron pan is perfect.)

✳ Lightly butter both sides of each bun. Place in the skillet and cook for about 2 minutes until golden brown. Turn the buns over and toast the other side. Or, toast the buns under a broiler instead.

✳ When the buns are ready, stuff them with the chilled lobster salad. Place each roll on a small paper or China plate; accompany with pickles and potato chips. Serve at once.

MAKES 6 ROLLS

IN THE summertime, ROADSIDE STANDS DOT THE COAST OF MAINE OFFERING SANDWICHES OF FRESH COOL LOBSTER SALAD ON BUTTERY grilled NEW ENGLAND-STYLE BUNS, WHICH ARE SLIT ON THE SIDE, RATHER THAN IN THE middle.

SIDES AND ACCOMPANIMENTS

Smoky Ratatouille for a Crowd

CHRIS SCHLESINGER / REPRINTED FROM *LICENSE TO GRILL* (WILLIAM MORROW AND COMPANY)

2 medium yellow squash, cut lengthwise
   into planks about 1 inch thick

2 medium zucchini, cut lengthwise into
   planks about 1 inch thick

2 medium eggplants, cut lengthwise into
   planks about 1 inch thick

2 red onions, peeled and cut into rings
   about 1 inch thick

6 plum tomatoes, halved

3 red bell peppers, halved and seeded

1 pound large white mushrooms,
   trimmed and cleaned

3/4 cup vegetable oil

Salt and freshly cracked black pepper
   to taste

3/4 cup balsamic vinegar

1/2 cup olive oil

2 tablespoons minced garlic

1 cup roughly chopped mixed fresh herbs:
   parsley, basil, oregano, rosemary,
   thyme, and/or sage

✱ In a large bowl, combine all of the vegetables with the vegetable oil and salt and pepper to taste and toss well.

✱ Place the vegetables on the grill over a medium-hot fire and cook until they are golden brown and tender. You will have to keep a careful eye on the grill, because with all of the different shapes and sizes, the vegetables are going to be finishing at different times: It will take 4 to 5 minutes per side for the squash, zucchini, onions, and eggplant; 6 to 9 minutes total for the tomatoes; 5 to 7 minutes per side for the bell peppers; and 8 to 10 minutes total for the mushrooms.

✱ As you remove the cooked vegetables from the grill, set them aside to cool a bit. As soon as they are cool enough to handle, cut them into bite-sized pieces and place in a large bowl. Add the vinegar, olive oil, garlic, and herbs and toss gently. Season to taste with salt and pepper and serve warm or cold.

SERVES ABOUT 10

CHRIS'S version OF RATATOUILLE, THE FRENCH provincial VEGETABLE RAGOUT, GETS ITS SMOKY CHARACTER FROM COOKING THE SQUASH, EGGPLANT, PEPPERS, onions, AND tomatoes OVER A CHARCOAL GRILL.

SERVES 6 TO 8

IF YOU WANT TO SERVE AN

uncomplicated AND

EYE-APPEALING SIDE DISH,

THIS IS IT. CLEVER CUTS TURN

THE ZUCCHINI INTO A fan.

Parmesan-Crusted Zucchini Fans

SHIRLEY CORRIHER / REPRINTED FROM *COOKWISE* (WILLIAM MORROW AND COMPANY)

8 small zucchini, scrubbed
3 tablespoons butter, melted
$1/2$ teaspoon salt

$1/4$ teaspoon freshly grated nutmeg
1 cup freshly grated Parmesan cheese

✳ Preheat the broiler. Spray a baking sheet with nonstick cooking spray.

✳ Cut four or five slits lengthwise in each zucchini to within $1/2$ inch of the stem end. Steam the zucchini in a steamer or large pot with a steamer basket until just soft enough to bend without breaking, about 4 minutes.

✳ Spread each zucchini out on a baking sheet like a fan. Brush lightly with melted butter and sprinkle with salt and nutmeg. Generously cover each fan with Parmesan cheese. Slide the zucchini under the broiler until the cheese melts and is lightly browned. Serve hot.

Harvest Casserole

SUSAN WESTMORELAND / REPRINTED FROM *THE GOOD HOUSEKEEPING STEP-BY-STEP COOKBOOK*
(WILLIAM MORROW AND COMPANY)

5 tablespoons margarine or butter
1 jumbo onion (about 1 pound), cut into
    1/4-inch-thick slices
2 cloves garlic, minced
6 medium carrots (about 1 pound),
    peeled and thinly sliced
6 medium parsnips (about 1 pound),
    peeled and thinly sliced
1 small rutabaga (about 1 pound), peeled,
    cut into quarters, and thinly sliced

3 tablespoons all-purpose flour
1 1/2 teaspoons salt
1/4 teaspoon coarsely ground black
    pepper
1/4 teaspoon ground nutmeg
2 1/2 cups milk
1/4 cup freshly grated Parmesan cheese
Chopped fresh parsley for garnish

✳ Preheat the oven to 375°F. In a nonstick 10-inch skillet, melt 3 tablespoons of the margarine over medium heat. Add the onion and garlic; cook 15 to 20 minutes, stirring often, until golden.

✳ In a shallow 2½-quart casserole, toss the carrots, parsnips, rutabaga, and the onion mixture until well combined. Cover the casserole and bake 45 minutes, or until the vegetables are fork-tender.

✳ Meanwhile, in a 2-quart saucepan, melt the remaining 2 tablespoons margarine over medium heat. Stir in the flour, salt, pepper, and nutmeg; cook, stirring, 1 minute.

✳ Gradually stir the milk into the flour mixture in the saucepan; cook, stirring constantly, until the sauce thickens slightly and boils.

✳ Stir the sauce into vegetables. Sprinkle grated Parmesan cheese evenly over the top. Bake the casserole, uncovered, 15 minutes longer, or until the sauce is bubbly and the top is golden brown. To serve, sprinkle with parsley.

SERVES 8

CELEBRATE THE HARVEST WITH THIS autumn casserole. ANY ROOT VEGETABLE WOULD SUIT THIS PREPARATION — USE YOUR imagination. BEETS, TURNIPS, CELERY ROOT, AND SUNCHOKES (JERUSALEM ARTICHOKES) ARE fine ALTERNATES.

Creamed Spinach

COLMAN ANDREWS / REPRINTED FROM *SAVÈUR COOKS AUTHENTIC AMERICAN* **(CHRONICLE BOOKS)**

SERVES 4

COMPANY MAY WONDER WHY THIS creamed SPINACH TASTES BETTER THAN USUAL. ACCEPT THE compliment AND SMILE KNOWINGLY — A DASH OF ANISE-FLAVORED PERNOD LIQUEUR ADDS A NEW dimension.

2 pounds fresh spinach, trimmed
Salt
1 tablespoon butter
1 shallot, minced
2 teaspoons Pernod

2 teaspoons flour
2/3 cup half-and-half
Pinch freshly ground nutmeg
Freshly ground black pepper to taste

✸ Wash spinach thoroughly, then put it, with washing water still clinging to its leaves, in a large pot over medium heat. Sprinkle with salt and cook, stirring occasionally, until the spinach has wilted to one quarter of its volume, 3 to 5 minutes.

✸ Drain the spinach in a colander and cool under cold running water. Squeeze out the excess water and roughly chop.

✸ Melt the butter in a skillet over medium-low heat, add the shallot and cook until soft, about 10 minutes. Add the Pernod, then stir in the flour with a wooden spoon or a small whisk and cook 1 to 2 minutes to eliminate the raw flour taste. Stir in the half-and-half and, when heated through, add the spinach and nutmeg. Cook, stirring occasionally, until the creamed spinach is thick, about 3 minutes. Season to taste with salt and pepper.

Zucchini Ribbons with Mint

SUSAN WESTMORELAND / REPRINTED FROM *THE GOOD HOUSEKEEPING STEP-BY-STEP COOKBOOK*
(WILLIAM MORROW AND COMPANY)

4 very small zucchini (4 ounces each) or
   2 medium zucchini (8 ounces each)
1 tablespoon olive oil
2 cloves garlic, crushed with the side of
   a knife

$^1/_2$ teaspoon salt
2 tablespoons chopped fresh mint
Mint sprig for garnish

✶ Trim the ends from the zucchini. With a vegetable peeler or adjustable-blade slicer, shave the zucchini lengthwise into long strips (if the zucchini are wider than the peeler, first cut each lengthwise in half).

✶ In a 12-inch skillet, heat the olive oil with the garlic over medium heat until the garlic is golden; discard garlic.

✶ Increase the heat to high. Add the zucchini and salt to the skillet and cook, stirring, 2 minutes, or just until the zucchini wilts. Remove from heat; stir in the chopped mint. Serve garnished with the mint sprig.

SERVES 4

YOUR VEGETABLE PEELER . DOUBLES AS A slicer TO CUT ZUCCHINI INTO LONG decorative STRIPS FOR AN ATTRACTIVE SIDE DISH. FRESH mint GIVES IT A BOOST.

Gratin of Yukon Gold Potatoes

LAURIE BURROWS GRAD / REPRINTED FROM *ENTERTAINING LIGHT AND EASY* (SIMON & SCHUSTER)

SERVES 4 TO 6

YUKON GOLD POTATOES LOOK AND taste LIKE THEY HAVE BEEN BATHED IN butter. SUBSTITUTE RUSSET POTATOES IN A PINCH. LEAVE THE POTATOES UNPEELED, AS THE PEELS CONTAIN MANY NUTRIENTS AND ADD AN APPEALING RUSTIC texture TO THE DISH.

2 pounds Yukon gold or yellow Finnish potatoes, scrubbed clean and thinly sliced
1 large onion, thinly sliced
1 clove garlic, finely minced
3 tablespoons all-purpose flour

1/4 cup grated Jarlsberg Lite or other light Swiss cheese
Salt and freshly ground pepper to taste
1 1/3 cups defatted chicken or vegetable broth
3 tablespoons freshly grated Parmesan cheese

✳ Preheat the oven to 375°F. Generously coat a 1½-quart flat oval gratin, or similar-shaped baking dish, with olive oil nonstick cooking spray.

✳ In a large bowl, toss the potatoes, onion, and garlic with the flour, cheese, and salt and pepper until well coated.

✳ Layer the coated potatoes and onion slices in the prepared baking dish. Lightly spray the potatoes with olive oil nonstick cooking spray, pour the chicken or vegetable broth over the potatoes, and bake for 1¼ hours.

✳ Sprinkle the top evenly with the Parmesan cheese, and continue to bake for an additional 15 to 20 minutes, or until the potatoes are tender and the top is golden brown.

VARIATION: Reduced-fat cheddar, Monterey Jack, or Muenster cheese can be substituted for the Swiss.

POTATO gratins ARE
A FAVORITE OF THE FRENCH
KITCHEN. RAFAEL'S VERSION
USES chipotle PEPPERS
(SMOKED JALAPEÑOS)
AND FRESH CILANTRO FOR
A decidedly NEW
WORLD DISH.

Potato-Chipotle Gratin

RAFAEL PALOMINO / REPRINTED FROM *BISTRO LATINO* (WILLIAM MORROW AND COMPANY)

2 pounds Idaho potatoes, very thinly sliced
 (peeling is optional)
1¹/₄ cups crème fraiche or heavy cream
2 small cloves garlic, minced
1 teaspoon chipotle puree, or more to taste

1 cup grated manchego, Gruyère, or
 Swiss cheese
2 tablespoons finely chopped cilantro
 leaves or chives

✳ Preheat the oven to 350°F. Arrange half of the potatoes in a greased 6-cup baking dish. In a small bowl, combine the crème fraiche, garlic, and chipotle puree and mix well. Spread half of the mixture evenly over the potatoes. Sprinkle with half of the cheese. Repeat with the remaining potatoes, crème fraiche mixture, and cheese. Bake, uncovered, until the potatoes are tender and the top is golden brown, about 1 hour.

✳ Check the gratin after 50 minutes; if the top is already brown, cover the dish with aluminum foil for the rest of the baking time. Let the gratin rest for 10 minutes before serving. Sprinkle with the cilantro and serve.

Crisp Potato Kugel

MARLENE SOROSKY / REPRINTED FROM *FAST AND FESTIVE MEALS FOR THE JEWISH HOLIDAYS*
(WILLIAM MORROW AND COMPANY)

6 medium baking potatoes, about
   3 to 4 pounds, peeled
1 large onion
2 large eggs
1 teaspoon salt, or to taste

6 tablespoons (³/₄ stick) nondairy or
   regular margarine or butter, melted
2 tablespoons matzah meal (*see note*)
2 tablespoons nondairy or regular
   margarine or butter

✻ Place the oven rack in the upper third of the oven and preheat it to 400°F.

✻ Grate the potatoes and onion in a food processor with the shredding disk or with a hand
grater. Place in a colander and drain well, squeezing out excess moisture. In a large bowl,
whisk the eggs, salt, melted margarine, and matzah meal. Stir in the potato-onion mixture until well combined.

✻ To bake, place 2 tablespoons margarine in a 9 x 13-inch baking dish. Melt in the oven or
microwave. Tilt the dish to coat evenly with margarine. Pour the potato mixture into the
dish and spread evenly. Bake, uncovered, at 400°F for 15 minutes. Reduce the oven heat
to 375°F and continue baking for 45 more minutes, or until the top is crisp. Cut into
squares to serve.

NOTE: For year-round potato kugel, substitute 2 tablespoons all-purpose flour for the
matzah meal.

SERVES 8

A TRADITIONAL JEWISH
PUDDING, KUGEL IS MADE
WITH **potatoes** OR
NOODLES. THIS POTATO
VERSION HAS A **tender**,
moist INTERIOR AND A
CRISPY CARAMELIZED TOP.

Giant Potato-Carrot Pancake

MARLENE SOROSKY / REPRINTED FROM *FAST AND FESTIVE MEALS FOR THE JEWISH HOLIDAYS* (WILLIAM MORROW AND COMPANY)

1/2 cup finely chopped scallions with tops
2 tablespoons chopped fresh parsley
3 medium carrots, about 8 ounces, peeled
4 medium baking potatoes, about
   2 to 3 pounds, peeled
1 1/2 teaspoons salt

1/4 teaspoon freshly ground black pepper
3 tablespoons vegetable oil
3 tablespoons nondairy or regular
   margarine or butter
Applesauce and/or sour cream, for serving
   (optional)

✳ Place the oven rack in the upper third of oven and preheat it to 450°F.

✳ Place the scallions and parsley in a large bowl. Shred the carrots and potatoes with the shredding disk of a food processor or by hand and add to the bowl with onion. Add the salt and pepper, and toss until well combined.

✳ Heat the oil and margarine in a 12-inch skillet (preferably nonstick) over medium-high heat. If the handle is not ovenproof, cover it with a double thickness of heavy foil. Add the potato mixture, pressing down and smoothing the top with your hands or a spatula. Cover and cook for 7 to 10 minutes, or until the bottom is golden brown. Lift with a spatula from time to time to loosen the bottom and make sure it does not burn. If the pancake browns too quickly or slowly, lower or increase the heat.

✳ Place the skillet in the oven when the bottom is golden. Bake for 7 to 10 minutes, or until the top is firm. If desired, place under a broiler and brown the top. Remove the pancake from the oven and loosen the bottom with a spatula. Slide the pancake onto a platter or place the platter over the top and invert it. If not serving immediately, invert onto a baking sheet sprayed with nonstick cooking spray. The pancake may be cooled and held at room temperature, loosely covered, up to 4 hours. Reheat, uncovered, at 400°F for 10 minutes, or until crisp.

✳ To serve, cut into wedges and serve with applesauce and/or sour cream, if desired.

SERVES 8

RATHER THAN SERVING SEVERAL SMALL POTATO pancakes, MAKE ONE GIANT PANCAKE AND SERVE IT family-style. THIS METHOD OF PREPARATION SAVES time AND USES LESS COOKING OIL.

French Fries

COLMAN ANDREWS / REPRINTED FROM _SAVEUR COOKS AUTHENTIC AMERICAN_ (CHRONICLE BOOKS)

4 pounds russet potatoes, peeled	Peanut oil
	Salt

✳ Cut the potatoes into lengths about ¼ x ¼ x 3 inches (it is easiest to do this with a mandoline). Place the potatoes in a large nonreactive bowl, cover with water, and set aside in the refrigerator for about 2 hours.

✳ Pour the oil into a heavy-bottomed pot to a depth of 4 inches and heat over medium heat. Drain the potatoes, then dry very thoroughly with paper towels. Check the oil temperature with a kitchen thermometer. When the oil reaches 325°F, cook the potatoes, without browning, in small batches, turning occasionally, until they are tender and their edges are slightly crisp, about 4 minutes. Drain the potatoes on paper towels and allow to cool for about 20 minutes. Remove the oil from the heat. (The potatoes may be cooked to this point several hours in advance and kept in refrigerator until ready to crisp.)

✳ Reheat the oil. When the temperature reaches 375°F, fry the potatoes in small batches until crisp and golden, 1 to 2 minutes per batch. Drain on paper towels, sprinkle with salt, and serve.

SERVES 4

THE SECRET IS OUT — NOW YOU CAN MAKE perfect FRENCH fries AT HOME. BY FRYING THEM TWICE, YOU WILL GET THE SAME crispy AND golden BROWN POTATOES THAT YOU FIND IN YOUR FAVOR- ITE RESTAURANT.

All-Time Favorite Sour Cream Cornbread

SHIRLEY CORRIHER / REPRINTED FROM _COOKWISE_ (WILLIAM MORROW AND COMPANY)

3 large eggs
1¹/₂ cups canned creamed corn
1¹/₂ cups (about 14 ounces) sour cream
³/₄ cup corn, canola or vegetable oil
1¹/₂ cups cornbread mix or self-rising
  cornmeal, slightly packed

¹/₄ teaspoon salt
¹/₂ teaspoon baking powder
Nonstick cooking spray
3 tablespoons butter, melted

✳ Preheat the oven to 425°F.

✳ Beat the eggs slightly in a medium mixing bowl. Stir in the creamed corn, sour cream, and oil. Add the cornbread mix, salt, and baking powder. Stir to blend well.

✳ Spray a 9-inch skillet with an ovenproof handle with nonstick cooking spray (see note). Pour in the batter.

✳ Place the skillet on a burner over medium-high heat for 1 minute. Then place on a shelf in the upper third of the oven. Reduce the oven heat to 375°F, and bake for 35 to 40 minutes. Slide under the broiler, about 4 inches from the heat, for 45 to 60 seconds to brown the top. Watch carefully. Brush the top with melted butter for a shiny finish.

NOTE: Instead of a skillet, spray a 9-inch round cake pan with nonstick cooking spray. Pour the batter into the pan and place on a shelf in the upper third of the oven. Reduce the oven heat to 375°F, and bake for 40 minutes. Brown under the broiler as directed and brush with melted butter.

Sweet and Sassy Beans

JOHN WILLINGHAM / REPRINTED FROM *JOHN WILLINGHAM'S WORLD CHAMPION BAR-B-Q*
(WILLIAM MORROW AND COMPANY)

SERVES 8 TO 10

THESE BEANS TAKE ON A
FULL smoky FLAVOR
WHEN BAKED DIRECTLY ON
A SMOKER OR BARBECUE
COOKER. IF baking IN
A CONVENTIONAL OVEN, A
hint OF LIQUID SMOKE
WILL ADD pizzazz.

1/4 pound breakfast sausage or bacon, crumbled	1/4 cup Sweet Bar-B-Q Sauce (see *below*)
1/4 cup diced onion	1/2 cup molasses
1/4 pound smoked pork butt	1 1/2 tablespoons Mild Seasoning Mix (see *page 108*)
Four 16-ounce cans store-bought pork and beans	1/2 teaspoon liquid smoke (optional)

✱ Start a barbecue cooker, allowing it to reach a temperature of 250°F, or preheat the oven to 350°F.

✱ In a large skillet, cook the sausage and the onion over medium-high heat for 5 to 6 minutes until the sausage is browned and the onion is softened. Add the pork and cook for 2 to 3 minutes longer until the meat is just heated through.

✱ In a large bowl, combine the pork and beans, sauce, molasses, seasoning mix, and liquid smoke, if using. Stir well and transfer to a deep casserole. The casserole should be large enough to hold the mixture so that it is no deeper than 4 inches and no shallower than 2 inches. Add the sausage-pork mixture and stir well.

✱ Cook the beans in the cooker, uncovered, for 3½ hours, or in the oven, covered, for 2½ hours until hot and bubbling and the flavors are well blended.

Sweet Bar-B-Q Sauce

MAKES 2 QUARTS

SLATHER THIS tangy
sauce ON BARBECUED
MEATS AND POULTRY
AND PASS additional
SAUCE AT THE TABLE.

4 cups tomato sauce	2 tablespoons vegetable oil
1 1/2 cups cola, such as Coca-Cola or Pepsi or Royal Crown, or beer	1 tablespoon soy sauce
1 1/2 cups cider vinegar	1 tablespoon honey
1 1/2 cups chili sauce	1/2 teaspoon Tabasco sauce
1/4 cup prepared mustard	1 1/2 cups packed dark brown sugar
1/2 cup bottled steak sauce	2 tablespoons freshly ground black pepper
Juice of 2 lemons	2 tablespoons garlic salt
1/2 cup Worcestershire sauce	1 tablespoon dry mustard
	1 tablespoon butter or margarine

✱ In a large saucepan, combine the tomato sauce, cola, vinegar, chili sauce, mustard, steak sauce, lemon juice, Worcestershire sauce, oil, soy sauce, honey, and Tabasco. Stir well. Bring to a simmer over medium heat.

✳ In a small bowl or glass jar with a lid, combine the brown sugar, pepper, garlic salt, and dry mustard. Stir or shake to blend.

✳ Add the dry ingredients to the tomato mixture and stir well. Increase the heat to medium-high, stir in the butter, and bring to a brisk simmer, stirring frequently. Cook for about 20 minutes, or longer for thicker, more intensely flavored sauce. The longer the sauce cooks, the less its final volume.

✳ Cover the saucepan and reduce the heat to low. Cook for about 30 minutes, until the flavors are well blended. Cool to tepid. Use immediately or cover and refrigerate for up to 1 week.

Matzah Balls

MARLENE SOROSKY / REPRINTED FROM *FAST AND FESTIVE MEALS FOR THE JEWISH HOLIDAYS* (WILLIAM MORROW AND COMPANY)

4 large eggs
3 tablespoons vegetable oil or rendered chicken fat
1 cup matzah meal
1/3 cup chicken broth
1/4 cup finely ground almonds
1 1/2 teaspoons salt, or to taste
2 tablespoons finely chopped fresh parsley
1/2 teaspoon ground ginger (optional)
4 quarts salted water

✳ Whisk the eggs and oil in a medium bowl until blended. Stir in the matzah meal. Add the broth, almonds, salt, parsley, and ginger, if using. Stir to combine. Refrigerate 1 hour or more.

✳ With wet hands, form the mixture into 1 1/2-inch balls.

✳ To cook, bring salted water to a boil in a soup pot. Reduce to a simmer and drop in the matzah balls. Cover and cook at a low simmer for 20 minutes. Do not lift the lid while cooking. Drain and add the matzah balls to soup. (Matzah balls may be refrigerated in soup up to 2 days.)

MAKES ABOUT 28 MATZAH BALLS

STAPLES IN JEWISH CUISINE, THESE dumplings ARE PERFECT ADDITIONS TO steaming BOWLS OF CHICKEN SOUP.

Golden Onion Focaccia

SUSAN WESTMORELAND / REPRINTED FROM *THE GOOD HOUSEKEEPING STEP-BY-STEP COOKBOOK* (WILLIAM MORROW AND COMPANY)

1 package quick-rise yeast
1 teaspoon salt
About 2 cups all-purpose flour
4 tablespoons olive oil
1 cup water
1 cup whole-wheat flour
1 tablespoon yellow cornmeal

1 medium-size red onion, thinly sliced
2 tablespoons freshly grated Parmesan cheese
1 tablespoon fresh rosemary leaves, or 1 teaspoon dried rosemary, crushed
1/4 teaspoon cracked black pepper
Coarse salt (optional)

✱ In a large bowl, combine the yeast, 1 teaspoon salt, and 1 cup of the all-purpose flour. In a 1-quart saucepan, heat 2 tablespoons of the oil and the water over medium heat until very warm (120° to 130°F). With a mixer at low speed, gradually beat the liquid into the flour mixture just until blended. Increase the mixer speed to medium; beat 2 minutes. With a wooden spoon, stir in the whole-wheat flour to make a soft dough.

✱ Knead the dough in the bowl 8 minutes, working in about ½ cup more of the all-purpose flour. Cover loosely with plastic wrap; let rest 15 minutes. Grease a 13 x 9-inch metal baking pan and sprinkle with cornmeal.

✱ Pat dough into pan, pushing it into the corners. Cover loosely with plastic wrap; let rise in a warm place (80° to 85°F) 30 minutes, or until doubled in size.

✱ In a 10-inch skillet, heat 1 tablespoon of the oil over medium heat. Add the onion and cook until tender. Preheat the oven to 400°F. With a finger, make deep indentations 1 inch apart over the entire surface of dough, almost to the bottom of pan; drizzle with the remaining 1 tablespoon oil.

✱ Spoon the onion evenly over the dough and sprinkle with the remaining ingredients. Bake the focaccia 20 to 25 minutes, until golden. Cool 10 minutes in the pan or on a wire rack. Serve warm. Or, remove from the pan and cool completely to serve later.

OTHER TOPPINGS

Sweet pepper: In a 10-inch skillet, heat 1 tablespoon olive oil over medium heat; add 2 red or yellow bell peppers, sliced, and ¼ teaspoon salt; cook, stirring often, 15 minutes, or until tender.

Dried tomato and olive: Mix 6 oil-packed dried tomatoes, slivered, and ⅓ cup chopped, pitted kalamata olives.

SERVES 8

FOCACCIA IS rustic, PEASANT-STYLE ITALIAN FLAT BREAD TOPPED WITH VARIOUS SPICES, HERBS, OR VEGETABLES. THIS VERSION IS drizzled WITH OLIVE OIL AND SPRINKLED WITH SAUTÉED sweet ONIONS.

PASTA, RICE AND POLENTA

Macaroni and Cheese, The Canal House

MARIAN BURROS / REPRINTED FROM *THE NEW ELEGANT BUT EASY COOKBOOK*
(SIMON & SCHUSTER)

1 cup diced onion (about 4 ounces)

2 tablespoons unsalted butter

2 tablespoons unbleached flour

2 cups low-fat milk

1 tablespoon Dijon-style mustard

10 ounces extra-sharp aged white cheddar cheese, grated, plus 2 ounces, grated

Salt and freshly ground white pepper to taste

$1/8$ teaspoon ground nutmeg

$1/4$ to $1/2$ teaspoon hot pepper sauce

8 ounces cavatappi pasta

2 tablespoons grated Parmigiano-Reggiano cheese

✱ In a large saucepan, cook the onion over low heat in the melted butter until the onion is soft but not browned, 5 to 7 minutes. Stir in the flour. Remove from the heat and whisk in the milk until thoroughly blended. Return to medium heat and cook, stirring, until the mixture begins to thicken. Remove from the heat and stir in the mustard and the 10 ounces of cheddar cheese, the salt, pepper, nutmeg, and hot pepper sauce.

✱ Meanwhile, cook the cavatappi according to package directions until tender, but still firm to the bite, *al dente*. Drain, but do not rinse. Stir immediately into the prepared cheese sauce until well blended. Adjust the seasonings.

✱ Spoon the mixture into a 9 x 13-inch baking dish. Top with the remaining 2 ounces of cheddar cheese and the Parmigiano-Reggiano. Refrigerate, if desired.

✱ To serve, let the dish return to room temperature. Preheat the oven to 400°F. Bake about 30 minutes, until the mixture is hot, bubbling throughout, and golden.

**SERVES 3 TO 4
AS A MAIN DISH,
6 AS A SIDE DISH**

THE CANAL HOUSE, A RES-TAURANT IN MANHATTAN'S hip SOHO DISTRICT, USES A HIGH-QUALITY, sharp WHITE CHEDDAR CHEESE FOR THEIR take ON MACARONI AND CHEESE. OTHER corkscrew-shaped PASTAS CAN BE SUBSTITUTED FOR THE CAVATAPPI spirals.

Baked Maccheroni with Winter Tomato Sauce

LYNNE ROSSETTO KASPER / REPRINTED FROM *THE SPLENDID TABLE* **(WILLIAM MORROW AND COMPANY)**

SERVES 6 TO 8 AS A FIRST COURSE, 4 TO 6 AS A MAIN DISH

THIS version OF "MAC AND CHEESE" MAY WEAN YOU FOREVER FROM THE TYPICAL AMERICAN PREPARATION. LYNNE KEEPS WITH THE NORTHERN Italian TRADITION, PERSONALIZING HER MACCHERONI WITH LAYERS OF sautéed MUSHROOMS. ONCE YOU GAIN confidence WITH THE DISH, YOU MAY BE INSPIRED TO CREATE YOUR OWN SIGNATURE style.

4 tablespoons extra-virgin olive oil
1 pound small fresh button mushrooms
3 tablespoons minced fresh Italian parsley
Salt and freshly ground black pepper
1 large clove garlic, minced
1 recipe Winter Tomato Sauce (see page 53)
1 1/3 cups fresh peas, cooked, or frozen tiny peas, defrosted

1/2 cup heavy cream
6 quarts salted water
1 pound dried imported penne, sedani, or fusilli pasta
1/2 cup (2 ounces) Italian Parmigiano-Reggiano cheese
6 ounces mild Italian sheep cheese

✳ Heat 3 tablespoons of the olive oil in a 12-inch skillet over high heat. Add the mushrooms and parsley, and cook over high heat, uncovered, stirring frequently, 3 minutes, or until the mushrooms start giving off a little liquid.

✳ Sprinkle lightly with salt and pepper, then add the garlic. Continue sautéing, turning often, 8 minutes, or until the mushrooms are golden brown and all their liquid has evaporated. Allow to cool, and taste for seasoning.

✳ Combine the Winter Tomato Sauce, peas, and cream in a large bowl. Bring the salted water to a hard rolling boil. Drop in the pasta and stir to separate the pieces. Cook at a fierce boil for 12 minutes, or until the pasta is barely tender enough to eat, still a little underdone. Drain thoroughly in a colander. Fold the pasta into the sauce, along with the Parmigiano-Reggiano cheese.

✳ Preheat the oven to 350°F. Grease a 2 1/2-quart shallow baking dish with the remaining 1 tablespoon olive oil. Spread half of the pasta in the baking dish. Spoon all of the mushrooms over the pasta. Using a vegetable peeler, shave half of the sheep cheese over the mushrooms. Cover with the remaining pasta, then top with shavings of the remaining sheep cheese. The casserole can be assembled up to 24 hours before serving. Cover it and refrigerate. Let the casserole stand 1 hour at room temperature before baking.

✳ Cover the dish lightly with foil, and bake 40 to 45 minutes, or until a knife inserted in the center comes out warm. Uncover the dish and bake another 5 to 10 minutes, or until the cheese is melted but not browned. Serve hot in warmed soup dishes.

Winter Tomato Sauce

3 tablespoons fruity extra-virgin olive oil
1 medium onion, minced
1 small carrot, minced
1 small stalk celery with leaves, minced
3 tablespoons minced fresh Italian parsley
1 large clove garlic, minced
3 tablespoons chopped fresh basil leaves, or 2 fresh sage leaves and one 1/2-inch sprig fresh rosemary

1 tablespoon imported Italian tomato paste
2 pounds canned tomatoes with their liquid, or fresh tomatoes, peeled, seeded, and chopped
Pinch of sugar (optional)
Salt and freshly ground black pepper to taste

MAKES 3 TO 4 CUPS

CONSIDER THIS TOMATO SAUCE A staple TO KEEP ON HAND AS YOU WOULD MILK OR BUTTER. USE IT FOR RISOTTOS, lasagnas OR basic PASTA DISHES.

✳ Heat the oil over medium heat in a 3- to 4-quart heavy saucepan. Drop in the minced vegetables and parsley. Slowly sauté, stirring often, 10 minutes, or until the vegetables are golden brown.

✳ Add the garlic and the herbs, and cook only 30 seconds. Blend in the tomato paste and the tomatoes, crushing them as they go into the pot. Bring the sauce to a lively bubble and keep it uncovered as you cook it over medium-high heat 8 minutes, or until thickened. Taste for seasoning.

✳ The sauce can be made up to 4 days before serving. Cook, cover, and store in the refrigerator. Freeze the sauce up to 3 months.

Garganelli with Roasted Peppers, Peas, and Cream

LYNNE ROSSETTO KASPER / REPRINTED FROM *THE SPLENDID TABLE* (WILLIAM MORROW AND COMPANY)

4 medium-size red bell peppers

1 1/2 tablespoons unsalted butter

2 1/2 ounces thinly sliced Prosciutto di Parma, coarsely chopped

1 cup heavy cream

6 to 8 quarts salted water

1 pound fresh garganelli or imported dried penne rigate pasta

2 1/3 cups very sweet fresh peas, lightly steamed, or frozen tiny peas, defrosted

1 cup (4 ounces) freshly grated Italian Parmigiano-Reggiano cheese

Salt to taste

1/4 to 1/2 teaspoon freshly ground black pepper

* To roast the peppers, sear and blister them all over on an outdoor grill, or on a sheet of aluminum foil on an oven rack set about 3 to 4 inches below a preheated broiler. Keep turning the peppers until their surfaces are well seared. Then tuck the peppers into a plastic or paper bag, seal, and let stand about 30 minutes. Slip off the skins, core, and seed. Cut the peppers into 1/2- to 3/4-inch dice. The peppers can be roasted a day in advance, and stored in a sealed container in the refrigerator.

* Melt the butter in a 12-inch skillet over medium-high heat and sauté the prosciutto 30 seconds. Add the roasted peppers and cook another 30 seconds. Add the cream, and set aside off the heat.

* Have a serving bowl and shallow soup dishes warming in a low oven. Bring the salted water to a vigorous boil. Drop in the pasta and cook until tender, but still firm to the bite, *al dente*. Watch carefully; fresh pasta could cook in about 30 seconds, dried pasta will take 10 to 12 minutes. Drain the cooked pasta in a large colander.

* Quickly bring the sauce to a boil, stirring in the peas. Immediately add the hot pasta, and toss over high heat until the sauce has totally covered the pasta. Add the cheese, and toss to coat and penetrate. Add salt to taste, and lots of freshly ground pepper. Transfer to the heated serving bowl and serve in heated soup dishes.

SERVES 6 TO 8 AS A FIRST COURSE, 4 TO 6 AS A MAIN DISH

IF YOU ARE NOT able TO FIND GARGANELLI PASTA (RIBBED HOLLOW CYLIN-DERS), PENNE works JUST AS WELL. ALL OF THE colors OF ITALY ARE REPRESENTED HERE— GREEN PEAS, RED PEPPERS, AND WHITE PARMIGIANO.

Spaghetti with Fried Bread Crumbs, Pancetta, and Hot Pepper

BIBA CAGGIANO / REPRINTED FROM *ITALY AL DENTE* (WILLIAM MORROW AND COMPANY)

SERVES 4 TO 6

THIS SPAGHETTI dish IS PREPARED PEASANT-STYLE. THAT IS, INSTEAD OF USING EXPENSIVE CHEESE TO COAT THE PASTA, FRIED BREAD CRUMBS ARE ADDED FOR A terrific CRUNCHINESS. LOOK FOR pancetta (UNSMOKED, SALT-CURED Italian BACON) AT AN ITALIAN DELI OR GOURMET grocery.

Water
1 tablespoon salt, plus more to taste
1 pound spaghetti or spaghettini
1/2 cup extra-virgin olive oil
1/4 pound thickly sliced pancetta, cut into
    thin strips

3 anchovy fillets, finely chopped
1 large clove garlic, finely minced
Chopped fresh red chili pepper or hot red
    pepper flakes to taste
2 tablespoons plain bread crumbs
2 tablespoons chopped fresh parsley

✱ Bring a large pot of water to a boil. Add 1 tablespoon salt and the spaghetti. Cook, uncovered, over high heat until the spaghetti is tender but still firm to the bite, *al dente*.

✱ Heat the oil in a large skillet over medium heat. Add the pancetta and cook, stirring, until it is lightly golden, about 2 minutes. Add the anchovies, garlic, and chili pepper and stir for less than a minute. Increase the heat to high, add the bread crumbs, and stir quickly until the bread crumbs are lightly golden, 5 to 10 seconds. (Keep your eyes on the skillet because the bread crumbs will turn golden in not time at all.) Turn the heat off under the skillet.

✱ Drain the spaghetti and place in the skillet with the bread crumb mixture. Add the parsley and season lightly with salt. Toss everything well over low heat until pasta and sauce are well combined. Taste, adjust the seasonings, and serve immediately.

Tagliatelle with Caramelized Oranges and Almonds

LYNNE ROSSETTO KASPER / REPRINTED FROM *THE SPLENDID TABLE* (WILLIAM MORROW AND COMPANY)

1 quart water
3 large Valencia or navel oranges
8 tablespoons (1 stick) unsalted butter
1 1/2 cups orange juice
2/3 cup sugar
Generous 1/8 teaspoon freshly ground
    black pepper
6 quarts salted water

1 pound imported dried tagliatelle pasta
3 to 4 tablespoons sugar
1/2 to 1 teaspoon ground cinnamon
2/3 cup (5 ounces) freshly grated Italian
    Parmigiano-Reggiano cheese
1 cup whole blanched almonds, toasted
    and coarsely chopped

SERVES 10 TO 12

LONG ribbon-like TAGLIATELLE SUPPORTS THE sweet SAUCE COVERING IT. IN ITALY THIS dish IS SERVED AS A DESSERT OR SIDE DISH. IT traditionally ACCOMPANIES CHRISTMAS CAPON, PAGE 67.

✱ Bring 1 quart water to a boil. Using a citrus zester, remove the zest from the oranges in thin, long strips. Boil the zest for 3 minutes. Drain in a colander, rinse with cold water, and set aside.

✱ Melt the butter in a large skillet over medium heat. Using a wooden spatula, stir in about 1/4 cup of the orange juice and the 2/3 cup sugar. Melt the sugar in the butter over medium heat, frequently stirring in more spoonfuls of orange juice to keep the sauce form crystallizing (reserve about 1/3 cup for finishing the sauce). Once the sugar has dissolved, turn the heat to medium-high and stir occasionally as the mixture slowly turns amber, about 2 minutes. Once it reaches deep golden amber, blend in the pepper and two-thirds of the orange zest. Cook only a second or two, to protect the zest from burning. Step back from the skillet and, at arm's length, pour in the last 1/3 cup of the orange juice. It will bubble up and possibly spatter, then will thin the sauce to the ideal consistency. Turn off the heat. The sauce can be made several hours ahead; cover and set it aside at room temperature. Reheat to bubbling before adding the pasta.

✱ Have a large platter and dessert dishes warming in a low oven. (If you are serving this dish with the capon, the bird should be ready.) Bring the 6 quarts salted water to a boil in a large pot. Drop in the pasta, and cook until tender but still firm to the bite, *al dente*. Drain in a colander. Reheat the sauce to a lively bubble. Add the pasta to the skillet, and toss to coat thoroughly. Turn it onto the heated platter, and sprinkle with the 3 to 4 tablespoons sugar, cinnamon, cheese, almonds, and lastly, the remaining one-third of the orange zest. Mound small portions on heated dessert plates, and serve hot. Or, place the capon atop the pasta, and serve.

Pizza

SUSAN WESTMORELAND / REPRINTED FROM *THE GOOD HOUSEKEEPING ILLUSTRATED CHILDREN'S COOKBOOK* **(WILLIAM MORROW AND COMPANY)**

Toppings

1 green bell pepper, or ¹/₄ pound
    mushrooms, or ¹/₄ cup pitted large
    ripe olives, drained, or 1 ounce
    sliced pepperoni

Pizza

2 cups tomato sauce
1 teaspoon olive oil
1 tablespoon yellow cornmeal
One 10-ounce container refrigerated
    all-ready pizza crust
2 cups (8 ounces) shredded whole milk,
    part skim, or reduced fat mozzarella
    cheese
2 tablespoons grated Parmesan cheese

SERVES 8

THE KIDS CAN CHOOSE THEIR OWN toppings FOR THEIR PIZZA, JUST LIKE IN THE PIZZA PARLOR. THIS COULD BE THE perfect OPPORTUNITY TO COAX THEM INTO EATING vegetables.

✳ Decide that toppings you want on your pizza.

✳ If you want green pepper on your pizza, rinse it with running cold water. Pat it dry. Place the pepper on a cutting board. With a paring knife, cut it lengthwise in half. With the paring knife or your fingers, remove and discard the seeds and the white ribs. With the paring knife, cut each half lengthwise into thin strips. Set the strips aside.

✳ If you want mushrooms on your pizza, rinse them with running cold water. Pat them dry. Place the mushrooms on a cutting board. With a paring knife, cut off and discard the end of each stem. Cut each mushroom lengthwise into thin slices. Set the slices aside.

✳ If you want olives on your pizza, place them on a cutting board. With a paring knife, cut each one crosswise into rings. Set the rings aside.

✳ If you want pepperoni on your pizza, set the slices aside.

✳ To prepare the pizza, pour the tomato sauce into a saucepan. Bring it to a boil on the stove over high heat. Turn down the heat to low. Set the timer and simmer the sauce for 15 minutes. While the tomato sauce is simmering, preheat the oven to 450°F.

✳ Pour the olive oil into a 12-inch round pizza pan or 15½ x 10½-inch jelly-roll pan. Using a pastry brush, spread the oil on the bottom of the pan. Sprinkle the bottom of the pan evenly with the yellow cornmeal.

✳ Open the container of pizza crust. Gently unroll the dough and place it in the pan. Using your fingertips, press and stretch the dough to fit the prepared pan starting from the center of the dough.

(continued on next page)

✳ When the timer for the tomato sauce goes off, turn off the heat. Holding the handle of the saucepan with a pot holder, put the saucepan on a trivet. You should have about 1½ cups of tomato sauce left. Still holding the handle of the saucepan with a pot holder, use a ladle to spread the tomato sauce evenly over the dough. Stop spreading the sauce about 1 inch from the edge of the dough.

✳ Sprinkle the mozzarella cheese evenly on top of the tomato sauce. Now arrange the pepper, mushrooms, olives, or pepperoni, or a combination of toppings, evenly on top of the mozzarella cheese. Then sprinkle the topping with Parmesan cheese.

✳ Using the pot holders, place the pan in the oven. Set the timer and bake the pizza for 20 minutes, or until the crust is golden brown and the cheese is bubbling. Turn off the oven.

✳ Using the pot holders, remove the pan from the oven and place it on a trivet. Set the timer and let the pizza cool for 5 minutes. Holding the handle of the pan with a pot holder, cut the pizza into 8 portions with a pizza wheel.

Risotto with Roasted Red Bell Peppers

BIBA CAGGIANO / REPRINTED FROM *ITALY AL DENTE* (WILLIAM MORROW AND COMPANY)

2 large red bell peppers, roasted and
   peeled
6 cups vegetable broth or low-sodium
   canned chicken broth
4 tablespoons (1/2 stick) unsalted butter
1/2 cup finely minced yellow onion
2 cups imported Arborio rice or
   other rice for risotto

1/2 cup dry white wine
5 to 6 basil leaves, finely shredded, or
   1 tablespoon chopped fresh parsley
1/3 cup freshly grated Parmigiano-
   Reggiano cheese
Salt and freshly ground black pepper
   to taste

SERVES 4 TO 6

DEPENDING UPON YOUR
APPETITE, THIS RISOTTO
ACTS AS A delicate
ENTRÉE OR MOONLIGHTS
AS A lovely SIDE DISH.

✳ Cut the peppers into thin strips, then dice the strips. Place the peppers in a bowl, cover, and set aside until ready to use.

✳ Heat the broth in a medium saucepan and keep warm over low heat.

✳ Melt 3 tablespoons of the butter in a large skillet over medium heat. When the butter foams, add the onion and cook, stirring, until the onion is pale yellow and soft, 4 to 5 minutes. Add the rice and stir quickly until it is well coated with the butter and onion, 1 to 2 minutes. Add the peppers and all the juices to the rice and stir once or twice. Add the wine and cook, stirring, until it is almost all reduced. Add 1/2 cup of the simmering broth or just enough to barely cover the rice. Cook and stir until the broth has been absorbed almost completely. Continue cooking and stirring the rice in this manner, adding the broth 1/2 cup at a time, for 16 to 17 minutes.

✳ When the last addition of broth is almost all reduced, add the basil or parsley, the remaining 1 tablespoon butter, and the Parmigiano to the rice. Stir quickly for a minute or two until the butter and cheese melt and the rice has a moist, creamy consistency. Taste, adjust the seasonings, and serve.

Sherried Rice and Barley with Almonds

SHIRLEY CORRIHER / REPRINTED FROM *COOKWISE* **(WILLIAM MORROW AND COMPANY)**

2 medium onions, chopped
1 tablespoon canola, corn, peanut, or blended vegetable oil
2 tablespoons sugar
1 cup brown rice (*see note*)
1 cup barley (*see note*)

9 dried apple slices, chopped
4 cups water or chicken broth
3 tablespoons butter
2¼ teaspoons salt
3 tablespoons dry sherry
1 cup slivered almonds

✳ Sauté the onions in the oil in a heavy pot that has a lid over medium-high heat until soft. Sprinkle with the sugar and continue cooking for 1 minute. Add the rice, barley, apples, water, 2 tablespoons of the butter, 2 teaspoons of the salt, and sherry. Stir well and bring to a boil. Cover and cook at a low simmer for 40 minutes.

✳ While the rice is cooking, preheat the oven to 350°F. Spread the almonds on a baking sheet and roast until lightly browned, about 10 minutes. Stir in the remaining 1 tablespoon butter and ¼ teaspoon salt while the nuts are hot.

✳ Heat the rice-barley mixture an additional minute with the lid off and toss gently with a fork. Stir in half of the roasted almond slivers. Sprinkle the remaining half of the almonds over the top to garnish. Serve immediately.

NOTE: Both brown rice and barley are now available in 10-minute-cooking brands, which makes this a quick dish. Cook the grain and apple mixture for only 10 minutes in the first step.

Fried Rice

GRACE YOUNG / REPRINTED FROM *THE WISDOM OF THE CHINESE KITCHEN* **(SIMON & SCHUSTER)**

2 large eggs
6 ounces Chinese barbecued pork, store-
     bought or homemade (*see page 102*)
2 teaspoons vegetable oil, plus
     1 tablespoon
3 cups cooked brown rice, cooled

1 cup frozen peas, thawed
$1/3$ cup finely minced scallions
1 tablespoon thin soy sauce
$1/4$ teaspoon salt
$1/4$ teaspoon ground white pepper

✱ In a bowl, lightly beat the eggs. Cut the barbecued pork into ¼-inch dice to make about 1¼ cups. Heat a large wok over medium-high heat until hot, but not smoking. Add 2 teaspoons oil and beaten eggs, and cook 1 to 2 minutes, tilting the pan so that the egg pancake will be as thin as possible. When the bottom side is just beginning to brown and the egg pancake is just set, transfer to a cutting board. Allow the pancake to cool slightly and then cut into ¼-inch-wide and 2-inch-long strips.

✱ To the wok, add the remaining 1 tablespoon oil and rice, and stir-fry 2 to 3 minutes, breaking up the rice to separate the grains, until the rice is lightly coated with oil. Add the diced barbecued pork, peas, scallions, and egg strips, and stir-fry for 3 to 4 minutes until the rice is beginning to brown slightly. Add the soy sauce, salt and pepper and stir-fry for 1 minute. Serve immediately.

SERVES 4 TO 6

MAKING FRIED RICE IS A **practical** WAY TO REVITALIZE YOUR LEFT-OVERS. GRACE PREFERS THE TEXTURE OF BROWN RICE TO THE TYPICAL LONG-GRAIN RICE. TAILOR THE **ingredients** TO YOUR LIKING —YOU CAN SUBSTITUTE COOKED CHICKEN OR TURKEY FOR THE PORK OR ADD ANY TYPE OF **vegetables**.

Polenta Baked with Vegetables

MARION CUNNINGHAM / REPRINTED FROM *LEARNING TO COOK WITH MARION CUNNINGHAM* **(KNOPF)**

1 large red, ripe tomato	1 cup polenta, not instant
1 green bell pepper	3 1/4 cups lukewarm water
1 bunch fresh spinach, or 1/2 box (10-ounce box) frozen spinach, thawed	1 1/4 teaspoons salt
1 medium-size yellow onion	1/4 cup olive oil
	1/3 cup grated Parmesan cheese

✳ Preheat the oven to 350°F.

✳ Cut the stem off the tomato and chop the tomato into bite-size pieces. Cut the stem off the bell pepper and cut the pepper in half lengthwise (store one half for another use). Remove the veins and seeds and chop the pepper.

✳ If using fresh spinach, remove any large, tough stems, and wash the leaves. Take about half of the spinach, pile it on a cutting board and using a large knife, chop into pieces the size of large postage stamps. Press the leaves firmly into a measuring cup and measure out 1½ cups of chopped spinach. Wrap and store any extra spinach for another use. If using frozen spinach, be sure it is defrosted, and squeeze out any excess water with your hands.

✳ Peel and cut the onion in half lengthwise, from the stem-top down. Store one half for another use. Chop the remaining half of the onion.

✳ Put the polenta, water, salt, and olive oil into an 8-inch square baking dish and stir with a fork until blended. There's no need to grease the pan. Add the tomato, pepper, spinach, and onion to the polenta and stir to evenly distribute the vegetables. Put the baking pan on the center rack of the oven and bake for 30 minutes, then check to see if the liquid is boiling around the edges of the baking pan. If so, leave the temperature as is. If not, increase the oven heat to 400°F. Bake for another 15 minutes, or until the water has all been absorbed—that's your signal that the polenta is done.

✳ Remove the pan from the oven and put it on a heatproof counter. Sprinkle Parmesan cheese evenly over the top and let sit for 5 minutes.

✳ Cut the polenta into squares and serve warm.

SERVES 4 AS A MAIN DISH, 6 AS A SIDE DISH

THIS RECIPE WILL BECOME A favorite OF BOTH THE NOVICE AND TIME-RUSHED EXPERT cook. A FEW MINUTES OF PREPARATION followed BY THIRTY MINUTES IN THE OVEN WILL YIELD A satisfying, ONE-DISH MEAL.

POULTRY AND SEAFOOD

Christmas Capon

LYNNE ROSSETTO KASPER / REPRINTED FROM *THE SPLENDID TABLE* (WILLIAM MORROW AND COMPANY)

One 6- to 7-pound capon (organic free-range preferred)

1/2 lemon

Salt and freshly ground black pepper

1/8 teaspoon freshly grated nutmeg

One 3-ounce piece Prosciutto di Parma, coarsely chopped

1/2 cup dry white wine

1/2 cup dry Marsala wine

✳ Rinse the capon under cold running water. Pat it dry and trim away all visible fat. Rub it inside and out with the lemon, gradually squeezing out the juice. Sprinkle the cavity and all of the bird's skin with the salt, pepper, and nutmeg. Tuck the prosciutto into the cavity. Set the bird on a platter, lightly cover with plastic wrap, and refrigerate overnight.

✳ To roast the capon, preheat the oven to 325°F. Truss the capon if desired. Lay the bird, breast side down, in a shallow roasting pan just large enough to accommodate it. Roast 25 minutes to the pound (2½ to 3 hours), or until an instant-reading thermometer tucked into the thickest part of the thigh reads 170°F.

✳ After the first hour, begin basting the capon with one-third of the white wine. After 20 minutes, add another third. Wait another 20 minutes and baste the capon with the last of the white wine. Then begin basting with the Marsala, using a third at a time. Baste the capon every 20 minutes with the Marsala and spoonfuls of its own pan juices. If the juices threaten to fry or burn, add a little water to the pan. During the last 30 minutes of roasting, turn the bird over to brown the breast area.

✳ To serve, warm a serving platter in a low oven. Carve the capon by slicing the breast meat into thick pieces and dividing the leg meat into three or four pieces. Arrange the pieces on the platter. Skim the fat from the pan juices and pour the juices over the capon. Scatter the prosciutto pieces from the cavity over the sliced meat, and serve hot.

SERVES 6 TO 8

THIS traditional SIXTEENTH CENTURY CHRISTMAS BIRD MAY WELL TAKE ON A life OF ITS OWN WITH YOUR family. CAPON IS, ESSENTIALLY, A MALE CHICKEN, BUT IT IS LARGER IN SIZE AND richer IN FLAVOR. THE MEAT IS tender AND juicy AND STAYS SO FROM BASTING WITH sweet MARSALA AND DRY WHITE WINE.

On Video

Chicken Tandoori

NEELAM BATRA / REPRINTED FROM *CHILIS TO CHUTNEYS: AMERICAN HOME COOKING WITH THE FLAVORS OF INDIA* (WILLIAM MORROW AND COMPANY)

8 pieces bone-in chicken breast halves and legs (2½ to 3 pounds), skin removed *[with bones & fat removed.]*
2 tablespoons vegetable oil
⅓ cup fresh lime or lemon juice, plus 1 tablespoon
2 teaspoons paprika
1 teaspoon salt, or to taste
1 cup nonfat plain yogurt, whisked until smooth
5 to 6 large cloves garlic, ground to a paste in a mortar and pestle (1 tablespoon)
One 1¼-inch piece peeled fresh ginger, ground to a paste in a mortar and pestle (1 tablespoon)
1½ teaspoons ground cumin
1 teaspoon garam masala
1 teaspoon ground dried fenugreek leaves
Thinly sliced scallions (white and pale green parts), chopped cilantro leaves, lime wedges, and minced serrano peppers, for garnish

1st. Marinade

* Make 1½-inch-deep cuts across each chicken piece—3 on each breast, 2 on each thigh, and 2 on each drumstick. Combine 1 tablespoon of the oil, ⅓ cup of the lime *(lemon)* juice, the paprika, and the salt and rub it over the chicken pieces, making sure to reach inside the cuts. Let marinate, covered with plastic wrap, for 30 to 60 minutes in the refrigerator.

2nd. Marinade

* Combine the yogurt, garlic, ginger, cumin, garam masala, and fenugreek leaves in a large bowl, and add the chicken, making sure to cover the pieces *+ gashes* with the mixture. Cover the bowl with plastic wrap and marinate the chicken pieces for at least 12 and up to 48 hours in the refrigerator (see note).

* Remove the chicken from the marinade and discard the marinade. Combine the remaining 1 tablespoon each of the oil and lime juice. *Can add 1 or 2 drops of red food coloring for color — not flavor.*

* To grill, cook the chicken on a barbecue over medium-hot coals, turning and basting the pieces with the lime juice mixture a few times (the last time during the final 5 minutes of cooking), until the chicken is tender and no longer pink inside, 20 to 30 minutes, depending on the size.

Can brush w/ lime juice + oil mixture after cooking + before serving as a glaze.

Chicken Tikka Masala

NEELAM BATRA / REPRINTED FROM *CHILIS TO CHUTNEYS: AMERICAN HOME COOKING WITH THE FLAVORS OF INDIA* **(WILLIAM MORROW AND COMPANY)**

4 to 5 cloves garlic, to taste, peeled

1 large onion, peeled and cut into 8 wedges

2 to 6 serrano or jalapeño peppers to taste, stems removed, (optional)

One 1 1/2-inch piece fresh ginger, peeled and cut into thin slices

4 to 5 large, vine-ripened tomatoes, coarsely chopped

1 cup loosely packed fresh cilantro leaves, soft stems included

3 tablespoons peanut oil

1 tablespoon dried coriander

2 teaspoons ground cumin

1 teaspoon paprika

2 teaspoons ground dried fenugreek leaves

1 1/4 teaspoons garam masala

1/2 teaspoon salt, or to taste

1/4 cup nonfat plain yogurt, whisked until smooth

3/4 to 1 cup milk or half-and-half, to taste

1 recipe Chicken Tandoori (*see page 68*), meat removed from the bone and cut into bite-size pieces

Chopped fresh cilantro for garnish

SERVES 8

SIMMERING PRECOOKED CHICKEN IN garlicky TOMATO-ONION SAUCE WITH LOTS OF spices PERMEATES IT WITH FLAVOR. LOOK FOR GARAM MASALA, A SPECIAL INDIAN SPICE MIXTURE, IN specialty FOOD stores AND GOURMET GROCERIES.

✳ In the work bowl of a food processor fitted with the metal blade and the motor running, process the garlic, onion, and peppers until smooth by dropping them through the feed tube. Remove to a bowl. In the same work bowl, process the ginger, tomatoes, and cilantro until smooth. Set aside.

✳ In a large nonstick saucepan, heat the oil over medium heat and cook the pureed onion-garlic mixture, stirring, until fragrant and golden brown, 7 to 10 minutes. Add the pureed tomato mixture and cook, stirring as necessary, until all the liquid evaporates, 10 to 15 minutes. Mix in the coriander, cumin, paprika, fenugreek leaves, 1 teaspoon of the garam masala, and the salt, and add the yogurt in a steady stream, stirring constantly to prevent it from curdling, until it is absorbed into the sauce. Finally, add the milk, increase the heat to high, and bring to a boil.

✳ Carefully mix in the Chicken Tandoori and simmer over medium-low heat for 5 to 10 minutes to blend the flavors. The sauce should be of medium consistency. Add some extra milk or water if it seems too thick or cook, uncovered, over high heat to thicken the sauce. Garnish with the remaining 1/4 teaspoon garam masala and cilantro and serve.

Coq Au Vin (Chicken in Red Wine)

JEAN PIERRE BREHIER / REPRINTED FROM *INCREDIBLE CUISINE* **(TIME LIFE)**

1/2 cup all-purpose flour
1/2 teaspoon salt
1/2 teaspoon freshly ground black pepper
4 chicken breasts, bone-in, skin removed
   and cut in half
4 chicken legs, bone-in, skin removed and
   cut in half
3 tablespoons extra-virgin olive oil
1 cup pearl onions, fresh or frozen
1/4 pound small fresh button mushrooms
   (quartered, if they are larger than
   1/2 inch in diameter)

1 slice 97% fat-free smoked ham, cut into
   1/4-inch cubes
1 tablespoon chopped fresh garlic
1/2 cup brandy
1 tablespoon chopped fresh thyme
2 cups Cabernet Sauvignon or other
   full-bodied red wine
1/2 cup chicken stock
2 tablespoons tomato paste
2 bay leaves
Salt and freshly ground black pepper
   to taste
2 tablespoons chopped fresh parsley

✱ Combine the flour, salt, and pepper on a large plate. Dredge the chicken pieces in the flour mixture.

✱ In a large Dutch oven (with a lid), heat 2 tablespoons of the olive oil. Brown the chicken pieces in the oil until golden brown on all sides. Remove the chicken pieces and set aside. Wipe the pan clean with a paper towel.

✱ In the same pot, heat the remaining 1 tablespoon olive oil, add the pearl onions and sauté until golden brown. Add the mushrooms and ham and sauté for 2 minutes. Add the garlic, and, when fragrant, add the brandy and thyme and reduce for 2 minutes. Add the red wine, stock, tomato paste, and bay leaves. Bring to a simmer and add the chicken pieces. Cover and cook slowly for about 35 minutes, or until the chicken meat comes off the bone easily.

✱ Remove the bay leaves. Adjust the seasoning with salt and pepper to taste. Sprinkle with chopped parsley.

SERVES 8

WINE-INFUSED CHICKEN, PEARL ONIONS, AND WHITE MUSHROOMS compose THIS TIMELESS FRENCH BISTRO-STYLE STEW, WHICH IS superb SERVED WITH MASHED POTATOES OR EGG NOODLES. FOR BEST RESULTS, CHOOSE A WINE THAT YOU WOULD serve AT THE TABLE.

Cheddar-Crusted Chicken Breasts with Grapes and Apples in Grand Marnier Sauce

SHIRLEY CORRIHER / REPRINTED FROM *COOKWISE* (WILLIAM MORROW AND COMPANY)

SERVES 8 TO 10

SHIRLEY revitalizes

COMFORT FOOD AT ITS

BEST. SERVE THIS DISH AT

BOTH fancy DINNER

PARTIES AND SUNDAY

FAMILY gatherings.

1 medium onion, quartered
1/2 teaspoon dried sage
1 1/2 cups chicken broth
4 cups water
10 skinless and boneless chicken breast halves
Two 10 1/2-ounce cans beef consommé
2 tablespoons dark brown sugar
1/2 cup orange marmalade
1/4 cup cornstarch dissolved in 1/4 cup cold water

3 red apples (Rome or McIntosh), cored and cut into wedges
3 tablespoons lightly salted butter
1/4 pound cheddar with good orange color, grated (about 1 cup)
Sherried Rice and Barley with Almonds (see page 62)
1 small bunch Red Flame grapes, about 30 grapes
3 tablespoons Grand Marnier

✱ Bring the onion, sage, broth, and water to a boil in a large saucepan. Add the boneless chicken breasts. Bring back to a simmer, simmer for 2 minutes, cover, and remove from the heat. Let stand about 10 minutes. Remove the chicken breasts to a plate and cover to keep warm.

✱ Heat the consommé, brown sugar, orange marmalade, and cornstarch-water mixture in a large saucepan over medium-high heat until it reaches a slow boil, stirring constantly. Remove the sauce from the heat and set aside.

✱ Sauté the apples in butter in a heavy skillet over medium heat until just browned, 2 to 3 minutes on each side. Set aside.

✱ Heat the broiler. Spray a baking sheet with nonstick cooking spray. Dry the chicken breasts and place them on a baking sheet. Sprinkle each chicken breast with grated cheddar and slip under the broiler just to melt and brown the cheese.

✱ Mound the hot sherried rice and barley with almonds in the center of a large platter. Arrange the chicken breasts against the sides of the mound. Reheat the sauce and stir in the apple wedges, grapes, and Grand Marnier. Spoon the apples and grapes and a little sauce over the top of the mound, letting the apples and grapes cascade down the side of the mound. Drizzle some sauce over each chicken breast and serve.

Gus's Fried Chicken

COLMAN ANDREWS / REPRINTED FROM *SAVEUR COOKS AUTHENTIC AMERICAN* **(CHRONICLE BOOKS)**

One 3¹/₂-pound chicken, rinsed and
   cut into 8 pieces
1 quart buttermilk
3 cups flour
2 teaspoons paprika

1 teaspoon cayenne pepper
2 teaspoons salt, plus more to taste
1 teaspoon freshly ground black pepper,
   plus more to taste
Peanut oil

✱ Arrange the chicken pieces in a single layer in a nonreactive baking pan. Pour the buttermilk over the chicken, then cover and refrigerate for at least 2 hours, or as long as overnight.

✱ Combine the flour, paprika, cayenne, 2 teaspoons salt, and 1 teaspoon pepper in a large plastic bag and shake to mix thoroughly. Shake the chicken pieces one at a time with the seasoned flour in the bag until well coated.

✱ Pour the peanut oil into a large cast-iron skillet to a depth of ¾ inch. Heat the oil over medium-high heat until very hot but not smoking, and add chicken, largest pieces first, skin-side down. (Work in batches if your skillet won't hold all pieces at the same time.) Reduce the heat to medium and cook, turning once, until the chicken is golden brown and crispy, 12 to 15 minutes per side. Drain the fried chicken on paper towels and season to taste with salt and pepper.

SERVES 4

JUST OUTSIDE MEMPHIS YOU'LL FIND THE ORIGINAL GUS'S Fried CHICKEN. GUS WON'T REVEAL HIS FAMOUS RECIPE, BUT THIS ONE comes CLOSE. BE SURE TO BUY ENOUGH buttermilk, WHICH COULD BE THE SECRET TO HIS MOIST FRIED CHICKEN.

Chicken Fajitas with Mango Salsa

SAM GUGINO / REPRINTED FROM *COOKING TO BEAT THE CLOCK* (CHRONICLE BOOKS)

SERVES 4

FAJITAS ARE A TERRIFIC
MEAL FOR AN active
lifestyle. THIS FRESH
LATIN-STYLE SALSA HAS
CHUNKS OF MANGO AND
works EQUALLY WELL
WITH TURKEY, LAMB, PORK,
OR BEEF.

1 tablespoon sliced pickled jalapeño pepper, or 1 fresh jalapeño pepper
1 small sweet onion, such as Vidalia, or mild red onion, about 4 ounces
2 sprigs fresh cilantro
2 ripe but firm mangos
1 lime
2 tablespoons olive oil

4 boneless, skinless chicken breast halves, 5 to 6 ounces each, or 1$1/4$ to 1$1/2$ pounds chicken tenders
Salt and freshly ground black pepper to taste
2 medium-size red bell peppers
8 fajita-size flour tortillas

✱ Drop the jalapeño down the chute of a food processor with the motor running and puree. (If using a fresh jalapeño, stem and seed it first.) Stop the motor and scrape down the sides of the bowl with a rubber spatula. Peel and quarter the onion. Add the onion and cilantro leaves to the processor and pulse a few times.

✱ Place each mango, narrow side down, on a cutting surface. Slice through the mangos as close to the pits as possible on one side, then repeat on the other side. With a teaspoon, scoop out the flesh from the two thick slices and cut each slice into 4 pieces. Juice the lime. Add the mango and lime juice to the processor and pulse just until the salsa is fully combined but still chunky.

✱ Heat the oil in a wok or large, heavy skillet over medium-high heat. Cut the chicken into strips about ½-inch wide and 2 to 3 inches long. Season the strips with salt and pepper. Increase the heat to high and add the chicken. Cut the tops from the bell peppers. Stand them upright and cut down inside the four walls, separating them from the center core and seeds. Then cut the walls into thin strips. Add the strips to the chicken and cook, stirring periodically, for 5 minutes, or until the chicken is just done. The chicken should feel firm. (Cut through the center of one strip to check if you're not sure.)

✱ While the chicken cooks, spread the tortillas on a microwave-safe plate and cover with a paper towel. Cook in a microwave oven on high (100%) power for 20 seconds. Put the chicken and peppers on a small serving platter. Put the salsa in a small bowl. Bring the food to the table for diners to make their own fajitas. To assemble, put ⅛ of the chicken mixture on each tortilla, top with a tablespoon or more of salsa, and fold the tortilla over.

Garlic Shrimp and Pineapple Skewers

RAFAEL PALOMINO / REPRINTED FROM *BISTRO LATINO* (WILLIAM MORROW AND COMPANY)

24 jumbo shrimp, peeled and deveined
3/4 cup olive oil
3 cloves garlic, minced
1 tablespoon finely chopped fresh cilantro leaves
8 ounces guava paste
1/4 cup water
1 shallot, finely minced
2 teaspoons chipotle puree, or more to taste
2 cups peeled fresh pineapple chunks, or use canned

* If using wooden skewers, soak them in plenty of water for about 30 minutes. Combine the shrimp, oil, and garlic in a large bowl, mix well, and let marinate for 1 hour in the refrigerator. Place the cilantro, guava paste, water, shallot, and chipotle puree in a blender or food processor and process until smooth. Transfer to a large glass or ceramic bowl. Lift the shrimp out of the oil and add to the guava mixture. Add the pineapple and mix well. Marinate for another 5 to 10 minutes. Do not overmarinate the shrimp.

* Alternating with chunks of pineapple, thread the shrimp onto the skewers, folding each shrimp in half and pushing the point through both ends. Transfer the marinade to a small saucepan and simmer briefly.

* Meanwhile, heat a grill to very hot. Grill the skewers until the shrimp are just cooked through, about 2 minutes per side, basting frequently with the hot marinade. Serve immediately or at room temperature.

Tender Chicken on Rice

GRACE YOUNG / REPRINTED FROM *THE WISDOM OF THE CHINESE KITCHEN* **(SIMON & SCHUSTER)**

2 ounces Smithfiled ham
1 1/2 cups cold water
8 dried Chinese mushrooms
8 ounces skinless, boneless chicken breast
  or thigh, cut into 1/2-inch slices
2 tablespoons finely shredded fresh ginger
1 tablespoon Shao Xing rice wine
1 tablespoon thin soy sauce

1 tablespoon black soy sauce
1 1/2 teaspoons cornstarch
1/2 teaspoon sesame oil
1/4 teaspoon sugar
1/8 teaspoon ground white pepper
2 cups long-grain rice
2 tablespoons vegetable oil
1 scallion, cut into fine slivers

✳ Rinse the ham with cold running water. In a small saucepan, bring 1 cup of the water to a boil over high heat. Add the ham and return to a boil. Reduce the heat to medium-low, cover and simmer 20 minutes. Drain the ham and set aside until cool enough to handle. Slice the ham into paper-thin slices. Stack a few slices at a time and cut into slivers to make about 1/2 cup.

✳ In a small bowl, soak the mushrooms in the remaining 1/2 cup cold water for about 30 minutes to soften. When softened, drain and squeeze the mushrooms dry, reserving the mushroom liquid. Cut off and discard the mushroom stems and thinly slice the caps.

✳ Place the chicken in a medium bowl with the mushrooms, ginger, rice wine, thin soy sauce, black soy sauce, cornstarch, sesame oil, sugar, and pepper and mix with your hands.

✳ Place the rice in a 2-quart saucepan. Wash the rice in several changes of cold water until the water runs clear. Drain the rice. Level the rice and add enough water so that there is about 1 inch of water above the rice. Bring to a boil, covered, over high heat, never stirring the rice. Reduce the heat to medium-low and continue simmering, covered, 7 to 10 minutes or until the water almost completely evaporates.

✳ Meanwhile, stir 1 tablespoon of the vegetable oil into the chicken mixture and mix thoroughly. Heat a large wok over high heat until hot but not smoking. Add the remaining 1 tablespoon oil to the wok and carefully add the chicken mixture, spreading it in the wok. Cook undisturbed for 1 minute, letting the chicken begin to brown. Then, using a metal spatula, stir-fry 1 minute or until the chicken is lightly browned on all sides but not cooked through. Add the mushroom liquid, and ham, and cook, stirring, for 30 seconds.

✳ Uncover the rice and quickly spread the chicken and scallions over the top. Cover the pot and cook 5 minutes more until the chicken is cooked through and the rice is tender. Serve immediately.

Fifteen-Minute Bouillabaisse

SAM GUGINO / REPRINTED FROM *COOKING TO BEAT THE CLOCK* **(CHRONICLE BOOKS)**

8 tablespoons extra-virgin olive oil
1 medium onion, about 8 ounces
4 cloves garlic
1 large tomato, about 12 ounces, or
    one 15-ounce can whole tomatoes
Two 8-ounce bottles clam juice
2 teaspoons ground fennel
Salt and freshly ground black pepper
1/2 teaspoon saffron threads

3 pieces monkfish or swordfish, about
    4 ounces each
3 pieces halibut, snapper, or sea bass,
    about 4 ounces each
8 ounces cleaned squid bodies
1 small French baguette
1/2 cup roasted red bell peppers from
    a jar
1 egg yolk

✻ Preheat a broiler and adjust the broiling rack so it is 3 to 6 inches from the heat source. Heat 1 tablespoon of the oil in a large, deep, heavy skillet over medium-high heat. Peel and quarter the onion. Peel the garlic. Put the onion and 3 cloves of the garlic in a food processor. Pulse just until chopped. Scrape into the skillet, increase the heat to high, and cook for 2 minutes.

✻ Meanwhile, core the tomato, put it in the food processor, and pulse until chopped. (If using canned tomatoes, drain the tomatoes and coarsely chop.) Open the bottles of clam juice.

✻ Add the tomato, clam juice, fennel, and salt and pepper to taste to the skillet. Over the skillet, crush 1/4 teaspoon of the saffron between your fingers. Stir well, cover, and bring to a boil.

✻ Meanwhile, cut each piece of fish in half. Reduce the heat under the skillet to medium, add the fish, cover, and cook for 5 minutes.

✻ Meanwhile, cut the squid into rings. Add the squid for the final 1 minute of cooking.

✻ While the seafood cooks, cut the baguette on the diagonal into nine 1/2-inch slices. Put 8 of the slices on a baking sheet and toast both sides in the broiler, 1 minute on each side.

✻ To make the rouille, drop the remaining garlic clove down the chute of the food processor with the motor running. Stop the motor and scrape down the sides of the bowl with a rubber spatula. Add the roasted peppers, egg yolk, reserved bread slice, and remaining 1/4 teaspoon saffron, crushed between your fingers. Puree, then, with the motor running, gradually add the remaining 7 tablespoons of the olive oil through the chute until the mixture has the consistency of mayonnaise. Season to taste with salt.

✻ Divide the seafood and broth among 4 soup plates. Spread the rouille on the toasted baguette slices and put 2 slices on top of each soup plate. Serve any remaining rouille in a small bowl at the table.

SERVES 4

FOLLOW SAM'S METHOD AND YOU CAN pull TOGETHER A TRUE FRENCH BOUILLABAISSE IN FIFTEEN MINUTES FLAT. ALL OF THE TRADITIONAL ELEMENTS ARE REPRESENTED HERE AND CAN BE quickly ASSEMBLED, BUT TIMING IS essential.

IF YOU HAVE CONCERNS ABOUT USING RAW EGGS, REPLACE THE egg YOLK IN THIS recipe WITH 1/4 CUP EGG SUBSTITUTE.

Baked Stuffed Lobster

JASPER WHITE / REPRINTED FROM *LOBSTER AT HOME* (SIMON & SCHUSTER)

SERVES 2 TO 4

AN ultimate CENTER-PIECE DISH, prepare THE STUFFING FOR THIS CELEBRATED NEW ENGLAND classic AT THE LAST MINUTE.

FOR A MEDIUM main COURSE, SERVE HALF OF A 2-POUND LOBSTER TO EACH guest. FOR A LARGE PORTION, SERVE A WHOLE 1½- TO 1¾-POUND LOBSTER. CONSIDERED DELICACIES, THE TOMALLEY AND roe ARE THE GREEN-COLORED LIVER AND THE ORANGE-COLORED EGGS, RESPEC-TIVELY, OF THE lobster.

8 tablespoons (1 stick) unsalted butter, plus 3 tablespoons, melted, for brushing
1 medium onion (5 to 6 ounces), finely diced
2 sprigs fresh tarragon, leaves picked and coarsely chopped (2 teaspoons)
2 sprigs fresh Italian parsley, leaves picked and coarsely chopped (2 tablespoons)

4 ounces peeled raw Maine shrimp or 4 ounces raw scallops or cooked crabmeat or lobster meat, cut into ½-inch dice
Kosher or sea salt
Freshly ground black pepper
2 live 1½- to 2½-pound hard-shell select lobsters
3 ounces Ritz crackers, oyster crackers or dried corn bread, crumbled

✳ Preheat the oven to 425°F.

✳ Melt 8 tablespoons butter in a 9-inch skillet over medium heat. Add the onion and cook for 5 minutes until soft but not browned. Stir in the tarragon and parsley. If using raw shrimp or scallops, add them with the herbs and cook for 1 minute. Remove from the heat and let cool slightly. If using cooked lobster or crabmeat, remove the pan from the heat as soon as you stir in the herbs; let cool and then add the lobster or crabmeat. Season with salt and pepper.

✳ With a Chinese or chef's knife, split the lobsters in half lengthwise. Remove and discard the head sac and intestine. Remove the tomalley, and roe if present, and place in a small bowl. Break into small pieces using a fork. With the back side of a knife, crack the center of each claw on one side only. Season the lobsters lightly with salt and pepper. On a large roasting pan or baking sheet, place the halves together to resemble a butterfly.

✳ The tomalley and roe are optional for the stuffing. If you want to include them, mix them into the seafood mixture. Gently fold the crumbled crackers into the mixture. Divide the mixture evenly between 2 lobsters. If you are serving 1 lobster per person, spread the stuffing over the center so the lobsters look whole again. Do not pack the stuffing tightly, or it will affect the baking. Brush 3 tablespoons melted butter over the exposed tail meat, stuffing and claws. Bake, using the following chart as a guideline, until the lobster is cooked through and the stuffing is crisp and golden. Serve at once.

Baked Stuffed Lobster Cooking Times (in a preheated 425°F oven)

1½ pounds	17 minutes	2 pounds	24 minutes
1¾ pounds	20 minutes	2½ pounds	30 minutes

New World Paella

RAFAEL PALOMINO / REPRINTED FROM *BISTRO LATINO* (WILLIAM MORROW AND COMPANY)

1 tablespoon olive oil
2 teaspoons finely minced garlic
2 cups long-grain rice
2 pinches saffron threads
2 pinches sazon Goya
5 cups fish stock, at room temperature,
    or salted water
2 pinches kosher salt
3 tablespoons seeded and diced
    ripe tomato
8 large littleneck clams, cleaned

12 mussels, cleaned
2 dry chorizos, diced
2 small fresh lobsters, about 1¼ pounds,
    rinsed and quartered (optional;
    see note), or additional shrimp
8 large shrimp, peeled and deveined
½ cup drained freshly cooked or canned
    black beans
2 tablespoons thinly sliced scallions,
    white and pale green parts

SERVES 4

RAFAEL TAKES COMMON SPANISH paella INGREDIENTS — RICE, SAFFRON, spicy SAUSAGE, AND SHELLFISH — AND ADDS PLENTY OF LATIN flair. LOOK FOR UNFAMILIAR LATIN ingredients, SUCH AS SAZON GOYA AND chorizos, IN A LATIN AMERICAN MARKET.

✳ In a large skillet with curved sides, heat the oil over medium heat. Add the garlic and cook, stirring, until softened, about 2 minutes. Add the rice and stir until each grain is completely coated with oil. Sprinkle the saffron and sazon Goya over the rice and stir. Add 3 cups of the stock and a pinch of the salt to the skillet. Bring to a simmer and simmer gently, uncovered, stirring occasionally. After 5 minutes, add the tomato and stir. Simmer 3 minutes more. The mixture should still be quite soupy; as the liquid is absorbed, add more stock ½ cup at a time.

✳ Place the clams in the skillet, gently pushing them down into the rice. After the clams have cooked for 3 minutes, place the mussels in the skillet, gently pushing them down into the rice. After this point, do not stir the mixture, but move it gently every so often with a wooden spoon to make sure it is not sticking to the pan. Add more liquid only sparingly, keeping in mind that the final product should be quite dry.

✳ After the mussels have cooked for about 2 minutes, add the chorizos, pushing the pieces down into the rice. Place the lobsters, if using, and the shrimp on top of the mixture. Cook until the rice is cooked through but not mushy, about 5 minutes more. Sprinkle the paella with the black beans and scallions. Serve from the skillet at the table.

NOTE: Make sure the lobster claws are held together with rubber bands. Wrapping your hand in a kitchen towel, lay a lobster belly down on a steady surface and hold it firmly around the tail. Push the tip of a knife into the flesh between the head and the neck to sever the spinal cord. Let stand 2 minutes. Turn the lobster over and use a large kitchen knife or shears to cut it in half lengthwise. Discard the black vein behind the tail and the stomach sac behind the head. Twist off the claws. Repeat with the remaining lobster.

Bacon-Wrapped Scallops with Potato-Mushroom Cake

ROBERT CLARK / EXECUTIVE CHEF, C RESTAURANT, VANCOUVER, BRITISH COLUMBIA

SERVES 4

DAZZLE YOUR GUESTS WITH
THIS unique DISH. IT'S
easier TO MAKE THAN
YOU THINK.
AT HIS waterfront
RESTAURANT IN VANCOUVER,
BRITISH COLUMBIA, ROBERT
USES "OCTOPUS BACON"
TO WRAP around
SUCCULENT SEA SCALLOPS.
AT home, LOOK FOR
OCTOPUS BACON IN A FISH
MARKET OR USE STRIPS OF
REGULAR BACON.

Sauce

3 cups pinot noir wine
1 cup port wine
1/4 cup balsamic vinegar
1/2 cup diced shallots
1 tablespoon unsalted butter
Salt and freshly ground black pepper
    to taste

1 1/2 pounds sea scallops
4 slices octopus bacon, grilled
1/2 pound shiitake mushrooms, sliced
1/2 cup milk

2 tablespoons unsalted butter
4 baking potatoes, cooked and run
    through a food mill
1/2 cup cream cheese
Salt and freshly ground black pepper
    to taste
20 spears asparagus, tough stalks peeled,
    cooked until tender-crisp and refreshed
    in ice water
10 baby beets, cooked and peeled
1 tablespoon unsalted butter

✳ For the sauce, place the pinot noir, port, balsamic vinegar, and shallots in a heavy bottomed pot and cook until the mixture is reduced and coats the back of a spoon. Whisk in the butter, season with salt and pepper and keep warm.

✳ Meanwhile, divide the scallops into 4 equal portions. Surround each portion with the grilled octopus bacon, securing the bacon in place with toothpicks.

✳ Sear the mushrooms in a nonstick pan over high heat until golden brown.

✳ Preheat the oven to 450°F. In a heavy bottomed saucepan, bring the milk and butter just to a boil. Add the potatoes and beat with a wooden spoon until light, fluffy, and hot. Mix in the cream cheese and cooked mushrooms and season with salt and pepper. Spread the potato-mushroom mixture into four 4-inch ring molds placed on a nonstick baking pan. Bake for 7 minutes. Keep warm.

✳ Sear the bacon-wrapped scallops in a hot skillet or on the grill, turning once, until the scallops are just done.

✳ In two small skillets, heat the asparagus and beets separately with 1/2 tablespoon each of butter until warmed through.

✳ Place a potato cake in the middle of each serving plate and top with a portion of bacon-wrapped scallops. Arrange the asparagus and beets decoratively around the potato cakes, dividing evenly. Drizzle a small amount of wine sauce around the vegetables on each plate. Serve immediately.

Salmon Fillet with Sweet, Grainy Mustard Crust

SHIRLEY CORRIHER / REPRINTED FROM *COOKWISE* **(WILLIAM MORROW AND COMPANY)**

2 cups apple juice

1/2 cup coarse-grain mustard

4 sprigs fresh dill, finely chopped

1 tablespoon oil

One 1³/₄-pound salmon fillet

1/4 teaspoon salt

1/8 teaspoon white pepper

Several sprigs fresh dill for garnish

✳ Preheat the oven to 375°F.

✳ Bring the apple juice to a boil in a medium skillet over medium-high heat and boil vigorously until reduced to less than 1/4 cup. (You really want only about 1 to 2 table-spoons of apple juice.) Stir the mustard into the reduced apple juice. Heat and stir until the mixture is the consistency of the mustard before you added the apple juice. Remove from the heat. Stir in the chopped fresh dill.

✳ Lightly grease a medium baking sheet with the oil. Rub the salmon with the salt and white pepper and place on the baking sheet. Coat the fillet with the apple juice-mustard mixture. Bake for 10 to 15 minutes, depending on the thickness of the salmon. Place on a serving platter, garnish with sprigs of fresh dill, and serve immediately.

SERVES 4

SWEET CONCENTRATED APPLE juice, GRAINY MUSTARD, AND FRESH DILL BOND AS A bold COATING FOR SALMON FILLETS.

BEEF, LAMB AND PORK

Chipotle-Rubbed Grilled Skirt Steak with Grill-Roasted Bananas

CHRIS SCHLESINGER / REPRINTED FROM *LICENSE TO GRILL* **(WILLIAM MORROW AND COMPANY)**

4 ripe bananas, unpeeled

1/4 cup canned chipotle peppers, mashed or chopped

1 tablespoon minced garlic

2 tablespoons cumin seeds, toasted if desired, or 1 tablespoon ground cumin

1/4 cup roughly chopped fresh cilantro

1/4 cup fresh lime juice (from about 2 limes)

1/4 cup peanut or vegetable oil

2 1/2 pounds skirt steak

Salt and freshly ground black pepper to taste

✳ Build a hot fire in your grill. Place the bananas around the edge of the grill so they are not over the flames. Slowly roast the bananas as you prepare the rest of the dish, about 12 to 15 minutes. They are done when the skin is brown and they are soft to the touch.

✳ In a medium bowl, combine the chipotles, garlic, cumin, cilantro, lime juice, and peanut oil.

✳ Sprinkle the skirt steak with salt and pepper, rub generously with the chipotle mixture, and grill over a hot fire for 3 to 4 minutes per side for medium-rare.

✳ To check for doneness, nick the steak and peek inside; if you like it more well done, continue to cook until it looks one degree less done than you like it. It will continue to cook a bit as it sits.

✳ Remove the steak from the grill and slice it thinly against the grain. Slice the bananas open so you can eat them right out of the skins and serve them along with the steak.

SERVES 4

SKIRT steak IS AN INEXPENSIVE CUT OF MEAT THAT CAN STAND UP TO STRONG, spicy FLAVORS. THE CHIPOTLE (SMOKED JALAPEÑO) RUB MAKES A fiery CRUST AND THE ROASTED BANANAS WILL DOUSE THE flames.

Grilled Steak Marinated in Citrus

RAFAEL PALOMINO / REPRINTED FROM *BISTRO LATINO* **(WILLIAM MORROW AND COMPANY)**

RAFAEL PALOMINO / REPRINTED FROM *BISTRO LATINO* (WILLIAM MORROW AND COMPANY)

SERVES 4

STEAK COMES ALIVE WHEN BRIEFLY SOAKED IN CITRUS JUICES AND **toasty** LAGER. A SHORT GRILLING TIME IS **all** YOU NEED TO COOK THE THINLY SLICED MEAT TO **perfection**.

Juice of 1 orange
Juice of 2 limes
3/4 cup lager beer, preferably dark and toasty, such as Negra Modelo
1 medium-size red onion, finely chopped
1 teaspoon kosher salt, or more to taste
2 pounds boneless sirloin steaks, not more than 1/2-inch thick, trimmed of fat
Freshly ground black pepper to taste
Lime wedges

✳ In a large glass or ceramic baking dish, combine the juices, beer, onion, and salt. Add the steaks, turn to coat both sides, cover, and let marinate in the refrigerator for 30 minutes.

✳ Meanwhile, heat a grill to very hot. Lift the steaks out of the marinade and grill just until both sides are well browned, 3 to 4 minutes total. Do not overcook; remember that the steaks are very thin. Season with salt and pepper and serve with lime wedges.

Brisket with Burgundy-Orange Sauce

MARLENE SOROSKY / REPRINTED FROM *FAST AND FESTIVE MEALS FOR THE JEWISH HOLIDAYS*
(WILLIAM MORROW AND COMPANY)

One envelope (about 1 ounce) onion
   soup mix
1 1/2 cups Burgundy wine
1/4 cup water
2 tablespoons flour
1 tablespoon dried basil
2 teaspoons dried thyme
1/3 cup orange marmalade

1 1/2 teaspoons grated orange peel
2 teaspoons sugar
4 cloves garlic, minced
1/4 to 1/2 teaspoon freshly ground black
   pepper, to taste
One 4-pound brisket of beef, trimmed of
   as much fat as possible
1 pound mushrooms, cleaned; if large,
   cut into halves or quarters

SERVES 8

LONG, slow COOKING
PRODUCES MEAT SO
tender YOU CAN CUT
IT WITH A FORK. BY ROAST-
ING THE MEAT EARLY AND
REFRIGERATING IT, YOU
CAN DO most OF THE
PREPARATION BEFORE THE
party. AT SERVING TIME,
ALL YOU NEED TO DO IS
REHEAT. THE COMBINATION
OF ORANGES, ONIONS,
AND WINE IS sublime.

✳ Preheat the oven to 300°F.

✳ Stir together the soup mix, wine, water, and flour until blended in a roaster into which the brisket fits comfortably. Stir in the basil, thyme, marmalade, orange peel, sugar, garlic, and pepper. Add the brisket, spooning some of the sauce over the top. Cover and bake for 4 hours, basting every hour until tender when pierced with a fork. If the sauce bubbles rapidly, reduce the oven heat to 275°F. Remove from the oven and place the brisket on a sheet of heavy foil. Pour the sauce into a bowl, cover, and refrigerate. When the brisket is cool, wrap in foil and refrigerate. The brisket and sauce may be refrigerated separately overnight.

✳ To carve, remove any solidified fat from the sauce and discard. Slice the brisket thinly against the grain. Overlap brisket slices in a shallow ovenproof dish that is just large enough to hold them. Pour the sauce over the meat. The brisket may be refrigerated, covered, up to 2 days or frozen. Defrost in the refrigerator overnight. Bring to room temperature before reheating.

✳ To reheat, preheat the oven to 325° or 350°F. Add the mushrooms to the meat, basting with the sauce. Bake, covered with foil, for 40 to 50 minutes, basting once, until heated through and the mushrooms are tender.

Tomato Beef

GRACE YOUNG / REPRINTED FROM *THE WISDOM OF THE CHINESE KITCHEN* **(SIMON & SCHUSTER)**

SERVES 4 TO 6

YOU DON'T HAVE TO WAIT
UNTIL tomatoes ARE
in SEASON TO MAKE THIS
UNCOMPLICATED STIR-FRY.
SERVED OVER RICE, IT'S A
FRESH IDEA FOR A quick
WEEKDAY MEAL.

8 ounces flank steak, well trimmed
1/4 teaspoon baking soda
1 1/2 teaspoons thin soy sauce
1 1/2 teaspoons cornstarch
1 teaspoon Shao Xing rice wine
1/4 teaspoon sesame oil
1 1/4 teaspoons sugar
1 1/2 quarts water

5 tomatoes (about 2 pounds)
1 teaspoon vegetable oil, plus
  1 tablespoon
6 slices peeled fresh ginger
3 tablespoons oyster sauce
1/4 cup cold water
4 scallions, cut into 2-inch sections

✱ Halve the flank steak along the grain into two strips. Cut each strip across the grain into 1/4-inch-thick slices. Place the flank steak in a shallow bowl and sprinkle with the baking soda; stir to combine. Add the soy sauce, cornstarch, rice wine, sesame oil, and 1/4 teaspoon of the sugar. Stir to combine and set aside.

✱ In a large pot, bring the water to a boil over high heat. Add the tomatoes and cook 1 to 3 minutes or until tomato skins just break. Remove the tomatoes with a slotted spoon and, when cool enough to handle, peel skins. Core the tomatoes and cut into 1/2-inch-thick wedges.

✱ Meanwhile, stir 1 teaspoon vegetable oil into the beef mixture. Heat a wok over high heat until hot but not smoking. Add the remaining 1 tablespoon vegetable oil and ginger, and stir-fry about 1 minute. Carefully add the beef mixture, spreading it in the wok. Cook undisturbed for 1 to 2 minutes, letting the beef begin to brown. Then, using a metal spatula, stir-fry 1 to 2 minutes or until the beef is browned but still slightly rare. Transfer beef to a plate and set aside.

✱ Add the tomatoes and the remaining 1 teaspoon sugar to the wok, and stir-fry 1 minute over high heat until the tomatoes begin to soften. Add the oyster sauce and cold water, cover, and cook 2 to 3 minutes or until tomatoes are just limp. Add the beef mixture and any juices that have accumulated on the plate and the scallions, and stir-fry 1 minute or until just heated through. Serve immediately.

Stuffed Beef Tenderloin

SUSAN WESTMORELAND / REPRINTED FROM *THE GOOD HOUSEKEEPING STEP-BY-STEP COOKBOOK* (WILLIAM MORROW AND COMPANY)

2 tablespoons vegetable oil
1 medium onion, minced
1 bunch (10 to 12 ounces) spinach, chopped
1/2 teaspoon salt
1/4 teaspoon ground black pepper
1/4 cup freshly grated Parmesan cheese
1/4 cup oil-packed sun-dried tomatoes, drained and finely chopped

One 3-pound center-cut beef tenderloin roast
1 beef-flavor bouillon cube or envelope
1/4 cup dry sherry
1 1/2 cups water
Chopped oil-packed sun-dried tomatoes, for garnish
Assorted sautéed vegetables (optional)

❋ Preheat the oven to 425°F. In a 12-inch skillet, heat the oil over medium heat. Add the onion; cook until tender and golden. Add the spinach, salt, and pepper; cook, stirring, until spinach just wilts.

❋ Remove the mixture from the heat; stir in the Parmesan cheese and 1/4 cup sun-dried tomatoes. Set aside.

❋ Make a lengthwise cut along the center of the tenderloin, cutting almost but not all the way through. Ease the tenderloin open. Spoon the spinach-cheese mixture evenly into the slit in the tenderloin, pressing firmly. Close the tenderloin, packing the spinach mixture into the slit.

❋ With kitchen string, tie the tenderloin securely in several places to hold the cut edges of meat together. Place the tenderloin, cut-side up, on a rack in a small roasting pan.

❋ Roast the tenderloin 45 to 50 minutes for medium-rare, or until desired doneness. After the meat has roasted 30 minutes, if necessary, cover the stuffing with foil to prevent drying out.

❋ Transfer the roast to a cutting board. Let stand 10 minutes; keep warm.

❋ Meanwhile, remove the rack from the roasting pan. Skim and discard the fat from the drippings; add the bouillon, sherry, and water to the roasting pan. Heat the mixture to boiling over medium-high heat; stir until the brown bits are loosened.

❋ To serve, remove the string from the beef; slice the beef. Arrange the slices on 10 plates; garnish with chopped sun-dried tomatoes and pass the gravy. Serve with sautéed vegetables, if desired.

SERVES 10

CONSIDER THIS easy OPTION FOR AN ELEGANT DINNER PARTY OR SUNDAY SUPPER. THE SPINACH AND DRIED TOMATO STUFFING MAKES A handsome PRESENTATION. UTILIZE THE PAN JUICES TO MAKE A LAST-MINUTE gravy FOR PASSING AT THE TABLE.

Rack of Lamb with Pistachio-Mint Crumb Crust and Tangy Mint Sauce

LAURIE BURROWS GRAD / REPRINTED FROM *ENTERTAINING LIGHT AND EASY* (SIMON & SCHUSTER)

SERVES 6

USE RIB OR LOIN LAMB RACKS FOR THIS DISH AND ASK YOUR butcher TO CUT THROUGH THE BONE CONNECTING THE RIBS.

FRESH BASIL, CHIVES, DILL, OR PARSLEY ARE lovely SUBSTITUTES FOR THE MINT IN THE sauce.

THE RACK OF LAMB CAN BE COATED EARLIER IN THE day AND KEPT REFRIGERATED UNTIL ready TO ROAST. ALLOW THE LAMB TO SIT AT ROOM TEMPERATURE FOR ONE hour BEFORE COOKING.

2 racks of lamb (1$^{1}/_{2}$ to 2 pounds each), very well trimmed of all visible fat

Coating Ingredients
1 cup dry white bread crumbs
3 tablespoons grainy Dijon-style mustard
2 tablespoons extra-virgin olive oil
2 tablespoons pistachio nuts, chopped
2 tablespoons finely chopped fresh mint
1 tablespoon finely chopped fresh parsley
1 tablespoon snipped fresh chives
2 teaspoons freshly minced garlic
2 teaspoons Worcestershire sauce
Salt and freshly ground pepper to taste

Mint Sauce
$^{1}/_{4}$ cup defatted chicken or beef broth
$^{1}/_{2}$ cup fresh mint, finely chopped (do not substitute dried)
3 tablespoons raspberry (or other sweet-tasting) vinegar
2 tablespoons snipped fresh chives
1$^{1}/_{2}$ tablespoons extra-virgin olive oil
Salt and freshly ground pepper to taste

Garnish
Sprigs of fresh mint

✳ Preheat the oven to 425°F. Place the lamb racks fat-side up in a roasting pan.

✳ Combine the coating ingredients in a bowl and mix until well combined. Pat the lamb dry with a paper towel and press the coating ingredients on top of the lamb, covering the entire surface.

✳ Roast the lamb for 25 to 30 minutes, or until a meat thermometer registers 135°F for medium-rare. Remove the racks to a platter and allow to stand for 10 minutes.

✳ Combine the mint sauce ingredients in a food processor and pulse until combined.

✳ Carve the lamb into chops and serve hot, accompanied by the mint sauce and garnished with sprigs of mint.

VARIATION: Substitute whole-wheat bread crumbs for the dry white bread crumbs.

Lamb Shanks with Portobello Mushrooms and Dried Cranberries

MARLENE SOROSKY / REPRINTED FROM *FAST AND FESTIVE MEALS FOR THE JEWISH HOLIDAYS* **(WILLIAM MORROW AND COMPANY)**

SERVES 6

1/2 cup flour

1 teaspoon salt

1/2 teaspoon freshly ground black pepper

6 lamb shanks, about 1 pound each, trimmed of fat

2 to 3 tablespoons vegetable oil

1 1/2 cups dry red wine

1 1/2 cups beef broth

1 1/2 cups cranberry juice cocktail

6 cloves garlic, minced

4 tablespoons chopped fresh rosemary

3 tablespoons flour mixed with 5 tablespoons red wine

One 12-ounce bag frozen pearl onions, not defrosted

12 to 16 ounces portobello mushrooms, cut into 1 1/2 x 3/4-inch strips

3/4 cup dried cranberries

One 12-ounce package extra-wide egg noodles, cooked according to package directions

Sprigs of fresh rosemary, for garnish (optional)

✳ Preheat the oven to 350°F.

✳ To prepare the lamb shanks, mix the flour, salt, and pepper in a large plastic bag. Add the lamb shanks, 1 or 2 pieces at a time, shake to coat, and pat off the excess flour mixture. In a large, wide, nonaluminum saucepan or Dutch oven, heat 2 tablespoons of the oil over high heat. Brown the lamb in batches, turning to brown all sides. If the drippings begin to burn, reduce the heat. If necessary, add more oil. Remove the lamb to a plate and pour off the fat. Stir the wine, broth, and juice into the pan. Bring to a boil, scraping up any brown bits. Stir in the garlic and 2 tablespoons of the rosemary. Return the lamb to the pan and bring to a boil.

✳ Cover the pan and bake for 1 hour. Rearrange the shanks, putting the top ones on the bottom, and bake for an additional 1 1/4 to 1 1/2 hours, or until very tender when pierced with a fork. Remove the lamb and immediately cover with waxed paper and foil and refrigerate. Refrigerate the sauce separately until the fat rises to the top and solidifies.

✳ To reheat the lamb, preheat the oven to 350°F. Scrape the fat from the top of the sauce and discard. Simmer the sauce for 10 minutes. Remove from heat and, stirring briskly, whisk in the flour dissolved in wine. Add the remaining 2 tablespoons rosemary and bring to a boil, stirring constantly. Place the shanks in a roasting pan and pour the sauce over. Sprinkle with the pearl onions, mushrooms, and cranberries, pushing them into the sauce. The lamb may be held, covered, at room temperature up to 4 hours. Bake, covered, for 1 hour, or until bubbling and heated through. Serve over cooked noodles. Garnish with sprigs of rosemary, if desired.

THIS LAMB COOKS up SO TENDER, THE MEAT WILL likely FALL FROM THE BONE. BRAISING IN tart CRANBERRY JUICE AND earthy RED WINE ENHANCES THE LAMB'S DISTINCTIVE flavor.

FOR EASY ENTERTAINING, MAKE THE LAMB SHANKS AND refrigerate FOR UP TO 2 DAYS BEFORE THE party.

Grilled Lamb Loin with Eggplant and Spiced Couscous Rolls

DENIS BLAIS / EXECUTIVE CHEF, THE PACIFIC PALISADES HOTEL, VANCOUVER, BRITISH COLUMBIA

SERVES 8

FOR YOUR next DINNER PARTY, CHOOSE THIS SIMPLE, elegant ENTRÉE. YOU CAN DO MOST OF THE PREPARATION AHEAD OF TIME AND assemble IT AT THE LAST MINUTE.

USE YOUR OWN FAVORITE RECIPE FOR TOMATO SAUCE.

Eight 4-ounce boneless lamb loins

Marinade
Juice and grated zest of 1 lemon
2 tablespoons chopped fresh rosemary
2 cloves garlic, crushed
2 tablespoons olive oil
1/2 teaspoon coarsely ground black pepper

Eggplant and Spiced Couscous Rolls
2 large eggplants, cut lengthwise into
   1/2-inch-thick slices
Olive oil for brushing
Salt and freshly ground black pepper
1 1/2 cups instant couscous

1/4 cup olive oil, plus 2 tablespoons
1 1/2 cups boiling water
1/2 cup diced mixed red and green
   bell peppers
2 shallots, minced
1/2 teaspoon chili flakes
1/2 teaspoon dried coriander
1/2 teaspoon ground cumin
1/4 cup coarsely chopped fresh parsley
2 tablespoons chopped fresh mint
1/4 cup dried currants
1/4 cup pine nuts, toasted

2 cups tomato sauce, warmed

✻ Put the lamb loins in a large shallow bowl.

✻ In a small mixing bowl, whisk the marinade ingredients together. Pour the marinade into the bowl with the lamb and mix to coat. Marinate in the refrigerator for 1 to 2 hours.

✻ To make the eggplant and spiced couscous rolls, generously brush the eggplant slices on both sides with oil and season with salt and pepper. Grill over a hot fire for 3 to 4 minutes per side. Lay out on a baking sheet to cool.

✻ In a mixing bowl, combine the couscous with 1/4 cup olive oil. Mix to coat all of the grains. Pour the boiling water over the couscous. Stir once, then cover the bowl tightly with aluminum foil and let stand for 5 to 10 minutes, or until the water is absorbed. Fluff the couscous with a fork to get rid of any lumps.

✻ In a heavy skillet, heat 2 tablespoons oil and sauté the peppers and shallots. Add the chili flakes, coriander, and cumin and reduce the heat to low. When the peppers are tender, transfer the mixture to the bowl with the couscous. Add the parsley, mint, currants, and pine nuts. Toss well and season with salt and pepper.

✻ Remove the lamb from the marinade and grill over a medium-hot fire for 4 to 5 minutes per side for medium doneness. Slice the lamb loins thinly.

✻ Spoon about 3 tablespoons of the couscous mixture onto each piece of grilled eggplant. Roll up and place in a baking dish. Bake in a 350°F oven until heated through.

✻ Spoon a small pool of tomato sauce onto each serving plate. Place two eggplant rolls on each plate and arrange the lamb decoratively on the side.

Barbecued Pork

GRACE YOUNG / REPRINTED FROM *THE WISDOM OF THE CHINESE KITCHEN* (SIMON & SCHUSTER)

SERVES 4 TO 6

AN EXCURSION TO YOUR

LOCAL ASIAN grocery

IS ONE WAY TO FAMILIARIZE

YOURSELF WITH THE SPICES

AND OTHER secrets OF

CHINESE CUISINE.

DON'T WORRY IF THERE

ARE leftovers—YOU

CAN USE THE juicy,

CARAMELIZED SCRAPS FOR

making SPRING ROLLS,

FRIED RICE, AND OTHER

CHINESE-INSPIRED DISHES.

2 pounds pork butt, well trimmed
4 tablespoons sugar
2 tablespoons thin soy sauce
2 tablespoons hoisin sauce
2 tablespoons black soy sauce

2 tablespoons Shao Xing rice wine
2 tablespoons ground bean sauce
2 teaspoons sesame oil
$1/4$ teaspoon ground white pepper
2 tablespoons honey

✳ Quarter the pork butt lengthwise. Rub the pork with 2 tablespoons of the sugar, place in a large bowl, and set aside for 15 minutes. Pour off the excess liquid.

✳ In a small bowl, combine the remaining 2 tablespoons sugar, thin soy sauce, hoisin sauce, black soy sauce, rice wine, bean sauce, sesame oil, and pepper, and stir to combine. Pour the mixture over the pork, making sure the pork is well coated. Loosely cover with plastic wrap and refrigerate overnight, turning the pork form time to time.

✳ When ready to roast, let the pork come to room temperature for at least $1\frac{1}{2}$ hours. Preheat a broiler. Place a roasting rack in a roasting pan. Add enough water so that the water reaches a depth of $\frac{1}{4}$ inch in the pan. Remove the pork from the marinade, reserving the marinade and, using your hands, spread the honey on the pork evenly. Place the pork on the roasting rack, leaving about 1 inch of space between the pieces.

✳ Carefully place the pan under the broiler (the pork should be about 4 inches from the broiler element) and broil until the meat is just beginning to char slightly, about 7 to 10 minutes. Monitor the water level in the roasting pan to make sure it never falls below $\frac{1}{4}$ inch. Turn the pork over, brush with the reserved marinade and broil until the meat is just beginning to char, about 7 to 10 minutes or until the pork registers 160°F when tested with a meat thermometer. If the pork is getting too charred, lightly cover the pork with a piece of aluminum foil.

✳ Carefully remove the barbecued pork from the broiler and set on a cutting board to cool 10 minutes. Slice the pork $\frac{1}{4}$-inch thick and serve warm or at room temperature with the meat juices.

Grilled Medallions of Pork with Sweet Potatoes, Cranberries, and Pine Nuts

MARCEL DESAULNIERS / REPRINTED FROM *THE TRELLIS COOKBOOK* (FIRESIDE)

3 pounds well-trimmed boneless pork loin, cut into 32 $1/2$-inch-thick medallions
$1/4$ cup olive oil
6 medium-size sweet potatoes, peeled
$1/2$ cup light brown sugar

$1/2$ pound (2 sticks) unsalted butter, softened
Salt and pepper to season
2 cups fresh cranberries
2 tablespoons granulated sugar
$1/2$ cup pine nuts

SERVES 8

A Japanese TURNING SLICER CUTS THE SWEET POTATOES INTO SPAGHETTI-like STRANDS. IF ONE IS NOT AVAILABLE, USE A LARGE KNIFE TO CUT THE sweet POTATOES INTO LONG, THIN STRIPS. THE STRIPS MAY TAKE A LITTLE longer TO COOK, HOWEVER.

✱ Coat the pork medallions with the olive oil and divide into 8 portions of 4 medallions. Individually wrap each portion with plastic wrap and refrigerate until needed.

✱ Trim the ends of the raw, peeled sweet potatoes so that the ends are flat. Reserve the ends. Cut the sweet potatoes into long, thin strands with a Japanese turning slicer. Reserve the uncut center sections. Place the sweet potato strands in a stainless-steel bowl with ice water to cover; refrigerate until needed.

✱ Cook the sweet potato ends and uncut center sections in 1 quart boiling salted water with $1/4$ cup of the brown sugar for 4 minutes. Drain and transfer to a bowl of ice water. When cool, drain thoroughly, then place in a food processor fitted with a metal blade. Pulse the cooked potatoes for 1 minute. Add the softened butter and salt and pepper to season. Pulse until thoroughly mixed. Transfer the sweet potato butter to a stainless-steel bowl, cover with plastic wrap, and keep at room temperature until needed.

✱ Preheat the oven to 300°F. Cut the cranberries in half. In a stainless-steel bowl, combine the granulated sugar and cranberries. Set aside until needed.

✱ Toast the pine nuts on a baking sheet in the preheated oven until golden brown, 10 to 12 minutes. Remove from the oven and hold at room temperature until needed. Lower the oven temperature to 225°F.

✱ Season the pork medallions with salt and pepper and grill over a medium charcoal or wood fire for 1 to 1½ minutes on each side. Transfer the medallions to a baking sheet, baste with half of the sweet potato butter, and hold in the oven while completing the recipe.

✱ Cook the sweet potato strands in 3 quarts boiling salted water with the remaining $1/4$ cup light brown sugar for 1 minute. Drain the cooked sweet potatoes in a colander and toss with the remaining half of the sweet potato butter.

✱ Portion the sweet potato strands onto each of eight warm 9- or 10-inch soup/pasta plates. Place 4 medallions of pork on each portion of sweet potatoes and sprinkle with cranberries and pine nuts. Serve immediately.

Maple-Glazed Roast Pork with Maple-Mustard Sauce

MARLENE SOROSKY / REPRINTED FROM *SEASON'S GREETINGS* (CHRONICLE BOOKS)

Glaze

1/2 cup vegetable oil
1/2 cup finely chopped onion
2 cups maple syrup
1/2 cup cider vinegar
3 tablespoons Dijon-style mustard
2 1/2 tablespoons dry mustard (Coleman's preferred)
1 teaspoon black pepper

One 4-pound boneless pork loin roast

Maple-Mustard Sauce

1 cup half-and-half
3 tablespoons dry mustard (Coleman's preferred)
1 tablespoon all-purpose flour
1/2 cup maple syrup
1/2 teaspoon salt
2 large egg yolks, at room temperature
1/4 cup cider vinegar
2 tablespoons Dijon-style mustard

Thinly sliced pumpernickel or rye bread

✹ To make the glaze, whisk the oil, onion, maple syrup, vinegar, Dijon and dry mustards, and pepper in a medium saucepan. Place the pan over moderately high heat and boil, stirring occasionally, until the mixture is reduced to 1¾ cups, about 20 minutes. Divide the glaze in half; refrigerate half for reassembling the cooked roast and use half for basting the roast during cooking.

✹ Preheat the oven to 425°F. Dry the pork with paper towels and remove as much fat as possible. Brush half of the reserved glaze over the entire roast. Place the roast on a rack in a shallow pan lined with foil. Roast for 30 minutes, brushing with some of the remaining glaze every 15 minutes. Reduce the oven temperature to 375°F. Roast for 35 to 45 more minutes, or until a meat thermometer inserted into the middle of the roast reads 150°F. Brush the roast with some of the glaze every 10 minutes. Remove the roast from the oven and cool to room temperature. Wrap it in foil and refrigerate until it is well chilled.

✳ To make the maple-mustard sauce, mix the half-and-half and dry mustard in a medium saucepan. Let the mixture sit 5 minutes to soften the mustard. Whisk in the flour, maple syrup, salt, egg yolks, vinegar, and Dijon mustard. Cook over moderate heat, whisking constantly, until the mixture comes to a full boil and thickens. Boil for 1 minute, whisking constantly. Remove it from the heat. Place the sauce in a bowl and cover with plastic wrap directly on the surface of the sauce. The sauce may be refrigerated, covered, for several weeks. Stir before using. Serve at room temperature.

✳ Slice the meat as thin as possible; do not be concerned if some of the pieces fall apart. Spread one side of each slice with the reserved refrigerated glaze and press the slices together, reforming the roast. Tie the roast with string to hold it together. Rewrap it in foil and refrigerate for several hours or overnight.

✳ Several hours before serving, bring the roast to room temperature. Remove the string and place the roast on a serving platter. Discard any juices that collect in the foil. Serve the roast at room temperature with desired sliced bread and maple-mustard sauce.

Willingham's World-Champion Ribs

JOHN WILLINGHAM / REPRINTED FROM *JOHN WILLINGHAM'S WORLD CHAMPION BAR-B-Q* (WILLIAM MORROW AND COMPANY)

2 slabs spareribs (6 to 7 pounds)
$^1/_2$ cup apple cider vinegar mixed with
   $^1/_2$ cup water

6 to 7 tablespoons Mild Seasoning Mix
   (*see below*)

✱ Lay the ribs in a nonreactive pan and brush on both sides with the vinegar-water mixture. Sprinkle with seasoning mix and rub it in with your fingertips, massaging it into the meat. Cover and refrigerate for at least 12 hours.

✱ Start the barbecue cooker, allowing it to reach a temperature of 250°F. Put the slabs in the cooker. (If the cooker is fitted with a rotisserie or carousel, attach the slabs to the apparatus.) Cook for 4$^1/_2$ to 5$^1/_2$ hours, turning the meat every 15 minutes (unless it is attached to a rotating apparatus). The ribs are done when the internal temperature of the meat reaches 180°F, when the ribs are flexible, when the meat is fork-tender, and when the ends of the bone extend about $^3/_8$ inch below the meat.

✱ To serve, cut the slabs into individual bones or 3-, 4- or 6-rib racks. Serve immediately with or without your favorite sauce.

✱ To store the ribs once they are cooked, let them cool to room temperature and wrap them in plastic wrap and hold at room temperature until ready to serve. Alternatively, hold the wrapped ribs in an insulated box for 2 to 3 hours, or refrigerate for a day or two. You can also freeze the ribs for up to a month.

✱ To reheat, puncture the plastic wrap and reheat them in a microwave for 2 to 3 minutes at high (100%) power, or, remove them from the plastic and heat them in a 300°F oven for about 20 minutes until hot.

Mild Seasoning Mix

2 tablespoons salt
1 teaspoon freshly ground black pepper
1 teaspoon lemon pepper
1 teaspoon cayenne pepper
1 teaspoon chili powder
1 teaspoon dry mustard

1 teaspoon dark or light brown sugar
$^1/_2$ teaspoon garlic powder
Pinch of cinnamon
Pinch of Accent or other flavor enhancer
   (optional)

✱ In a small bowl or glass jar with a lid, combine all the ingredients. Stir or shake to mix. Use immediately or store in a cool, dark place for several months. *Makes about ¼ cup*

James Beard's Roasted Spareribs

MARION CUNNINGHAM / REPRINTED FROM *LEARNING TO COOK WITH MARION CUNNINGHAM* (KNOPF)

4 pounds pork spareribs

2 tablespoons salt

1 tablespoon ground black pepper

✱ Preheat the oven to 350°F.

✱ To prepare and roast the ribs, rub the ribs with salt and pepper on both sides. Set a roasting or broiler rack in a roasting pan. Arrange the ribs on the rack, meaty side facing up. Put the pan on the center rack of the oven and roast the ribs for 30 minutes.

✱ Take the pan out of the oven, turn the ribs over, and roast for another 30 minutes. When the second 30 minutes are up, the ribs should be nicely browned and fairly crisp on the outside. If not, roast for another 10 minutes and check again.

✱ To cut and serve the ribs, allow 3 or 4 ribs per person and cut the rack of ribs into individual ribs and place on a platter or plates. Serve hot.

SERVES 4

YOU'LL LOVE THE rich FLAVOR OF THESE TENDER, MOIST RIBS. AS YOU WOULD expect FROM JAMES BEARD, THIS IS A "NO-FAIL" RECIPE THAT WILL BECOME AN ALL-TIME favorite IN YOUR HOUSE.

DESSERTS

Instant Strawberry-Peach Frozen Yogurt

**LAURIE BURROWS GRAD / REPRINTED FROM *ENTERTAINING LIGHT AND EASY*
(SIMON & SCHUSTER)**

1 cup plain nonfat yogurt	3/4 cup frozen strawberries
2 1/2 tablespoons honey	3/4 cup frozen sliced peaches
1/2 teaspoon pure vanilla extract	Strawberry halves for garnish

✳ Place the yogurt, honey, and vanilla in the work bowl of a food processor and process until just smooth.

✳ While the machine is running, drop the frozen fruit down the feed tube in a steady stream until it has combined with the yogurt into a smooth mixture.

✳ Garnish with strawberry halves and serve immediately.

VARIATION: Frozen unsweetened nectarines, raspberries, or other fruits can be substituted for strawberries and peaches.

SERVES 4

KEEP BAGS OF FROZEN UNSWEETENED FRUIT ON HAND IN THE FREEZER FOR dessert EMERGENCIES. BLENDED WITH YOGURT, HONEY, AND PURE VANILLA EXTRACT, YOU'LL CREATE A frothy, CHILLED SPUR-OF-THE-MOMENT DESSERT.

Brownie Puddle

ROSE LEVY BERANBAUM / REPRINTED FROM *THE PIE AND PASTRY BIBLE*
(CHARLES SCRIBNER'S SONS)

Brownie

1 cup pecan pieces or coarsely chopped
    pecans
14 tablespoons (1 3/4 sticks) unsalted butter
One 3-ounce bar bittersweet chocolate,
    preferably Lindt excellence, or Valrhona
    Caraque, broken into squares
1/2 cup plus 2 teaspoons (lightly spooned
    into the cup) unsweetened cocoa,
    preferably fine-quality Dutch-processed
1 cup plus 3 tablespoons granulated sugar

3 large eggs
2 teaspoons pure vanilla extract
One 3-ounce package cream cheese, cut
    into pieces
1/2 cup all-purpose flour
Pinch of salt

Ganache Puddle

2 ounces (2/3 of a 3-ounce bar) bittersweet
    chocolate (see above), coarsely chopped
1/3 cup heavy cream

✱ To make the brownie, preheat the oven to 325°F. Place one oven rack in the middle of the oven. Prepare a 9½-inch tart pan, with a removable bottom, by greasing the bottom then lining with parchment paper. Spray with Baker's Joy or nonstick vegetable spray. Place the pan on a cookie sheet to catch any possible leaks.

✱ Place the pecans on a cookie sheet and toast them in the oven, stirring occasionally, for about 10 minutes or until lightly browned. Cool completely.

✱ In a double boiler over hot water, melt the butter and chocolate, stirring 2 or 3 times.

✱ Beat in the cocoa, then the sugar, beating until incorporated. (If you are doing this by hand, use a whisk.) Beat in the eggs and vanilla. When incorporated, beat in the cream cheese until only small bits remain. Add the flour and salt and mix only until the flour is fully moistened. Stir in the nuts; scrape the batter into the prepared pan and spread it evenly. It will fill the pan almost to the top.

✱ Bake for 30 to 35 minutes or until the batter has set and a toothpick inserted 1-inch from the side comes out clean. The mixture will puff and rise a little above the sides, but will sink on cooling.

✳ While the brownie is baking, prepare the ganache puddle: Melt the chocolate in a microwave, using 15 second bursts on high (100%) power and stirring several times, or in a double boiler over hot but not simmering water, stirring occasionally. Add the cream and stir gently until the mixture is smooth and dark. If necessary (if the cream was too cold and the mixture not entirely smooth), return it to the heat until totally fluid and uniform in color.

✳ As soon as the brownie is removed from the oven, grease the end of a wooden spoon (½ inch in diameter) and twist slightly as you insert and withdraw it, to create 23 to 28 little holes.

✳ Using a small spoon to pour or a zipseal bag with a small piece of the corner cut, fill the holes with the ganache until slightly rounded (you will need at least ½ teaspoon for each).

✳ Place the pan on a wire rack and cool completely. The chocolate puddles will sink in as the brownie cools and more ganache can be added, to fill in any depressions, as long as the brownie is still warm enough to melt it. (If necessary, you can set the tart under a lamp to heat the ganache puddles and make them smooth.) Unmold by placing the pan on a canister smaller than the opening for the loose bottom and pressing the sides firmly down. To remove the parchment, refrigerate the tart or allow it to sit at room temperature until the puddles are firm to the touch. Cover a flat plate with plastic wrap, spray it lightly with nonstick vegetable spray and set it on top of the tart. Invert the tart; peel off the parchment, and reinvert it onto a serving plate.

✳ To serve, use a thin, sharp knife to cut wedges.

✳ To store, wrap the tart tightly in plastic wrap and store it in an airtight container at room temperature, or in the refrigerator or freezer; 1 week at room temperature, 1 month refrigerated, or several months frozen. Try eating it frozen or chilled if you like a chewy brownie, room temperature for a softer, creamier texture.

Chocolate Cashew Coconut Clusters

MARCEL DESAULNIERS / REPRINTED FROM *DEATH BY CHOCOLATE COOKIES*
(SIMON & SCHUSTER)

2 cups unsalted cashews
8 ounces shredded dried coconut

1 pound best-quality semisweet chocolate,
    chopped into $1/4$-inch pieces

✱ Preheat the oven to 325°F. Toast the cashews on a baking sheet in the preheated oven for 20 minutes until uniformly golden brown. Cool the nuts to room temperature.

✱ Toast the coconut on a baking sheet in the preheated oven until lightly golden around the edges, about 10 minutes. Cool the coconut to room temperature.

✱ Heat 1 inch of water in the bottom half of a double boiler over medium heat. With the heat on, place the semisweet chocolate in the top half of the double boiler. Use a rubber spatula to stir the chocolate until completely melted and smooth, about 5 to 6 minutes. Transfer the melted chocolate to a 4-quart bowl. Add the cashews and coconut. Use a rubber spatula to stir the mixture until the cashews and coconut are completely coated with chocolate.

✱ Immediately portion 24 clusters, 1 heaping tablespoon (approximately 1½ ounces) of mixture per cluster, onto wax paper. Allow the clusters to harden at room temperature for 1 hour, then refrigerate for 30 minutes until firm enough to handle. Store the clusters in a tightly sealed plastic container in the refrigerator until ready to serve. The clusters will keep in the refrigerator for several days.

**MAKES TWO DOZEN
2-INCH CLUSTERS**

COOKIE OR CANDY— CALL THEM WHAT YOU will. THESE CLUSTERS MAY JUST put YOUR LOCAL CANDY STORE OUT OF BUSINESS. BECAUSE THE RECIPE CALLS FOR A LARGE QUANTITY OF CHOCOLATE, top quality IS KEY.

LOOK FOR DRIED COCONUT FLAKES IN THE bulk food SECTION AT YOUR SPECIALTY GROCERY STORE OR MAJOR SUPERMARKET.

on Studio

Gooey Chocolate Peanut Butter Brownie Cake

MARCEL DESAULNIERS / REPRINTED FROM _DESSERTS TO DIE FOR_ (SIMON & SCHUSTER)

SERVES 12

ALL OF America's

FAVORITES ARE HERE—

chocolate, PEANUT

BUTTER, AND BROWNIES.

KEEP A CAREFUL EYE

ON THE cake LAYERS

WHILE BAKING TO ENSURE

A GOOEY TEXTURE.

Gooey Brownie Cakes

1/2 pound (2 sticks) unsalted butter, plus
    2 tablespoons, melted
12 ounces semisweet chocolate, broken
    into 1/2-ounce pieces
1 cup granulated sugar
3 large eggs
1 tablespoon pure vanilla extract
1/2 cup all-purpose flour
1 teaspoon baking powder
1 cup creamy peanut butter, room
    temperature

Chocolate Peanut Butter Ganache

1 1/2 cups heavy cream
3 tablespoons granulated sugar
2 tablespoons creamy peanut butter
18 ounces semisweet chocolate, broken
    into 1/2-ounce pieces

1 1/2 cups toasted unsalted peanuts,
    chopped into 1/8-inch pieces
    (see *note*, page 117)

✱ To make the gooey brownie cakes, preheat the oven to 300°F. Lightly coat the insides of three 9 x 1 1/2-inch cake pans with melted butter. Line each pan with parchment paper, then lightly coat the paper with more melted butter. Set aside.

✱ Heat 1 inch of water in the bottom half of a double boiler over medium heat. Place the semisweet chocolate and the 1/2 pound butter in the top half. Tightly cover the top with plastic wrap. Allow to heat for 8 to 12 minutes. Remove from heat and stir until smooth. Set aside until needed.

✱ Place the sugar, eggs, and vanilla in the bowl of an electric mixer fitted with a paddle. Beat on medium speed for 2 minutes. Use a rubber spatula to scrape down the sides of the bowl. Beat on high speed for 2 minutes. Scrape down the bowl. Add the melted chocolate and beat on medium speed until the chocolate is thoroughly incorporated, about 15 seconds. Add the flour and baking powder and beat on low for 1 minute. Remove the bowl from the mixer and use a rubber spatula to thoroughly combine the ingredients.

✱ Divide the batter between the prepared pans, spreading evenly. Place 1 of the pans on the center rack and the remaining 2 pans on the bottom rack of the preheated oven. Bake until the batter is set but not dry (a toothpick inserted in the center of the cakes should hold some residual batter) about 20 to 22 minutes. Rotate the brownie cakes from top to bottom about halfway through the baking time.

✱ Remove the brownie cakes from the oven and allow to cool in the pans at room temperature for 10 to 15 minutes. Invert each brownie cake onto an individual cake circle. (These baked brownie cake layers are very delicate, so use a knife to cut around the edges of the cake layers inside the pans; this will ensure that the cake layers do not tear when removed from their respective pans.) Remove the parchment paper from each brownie cake. Place the brownie cakes in the refrigerator to cool for 10 minutes. Remove 2 of the brownie cakes from the refrigerator and use a cake spatula to spread ½ cup of the peanut butter in an even layer over each cake. Place these 2 brownie cake layers in the freezer while preparing the ganache.

✳ To prepare the chocolate peanut butter ganache, heat the heavy cream, sugar, and creamy peanut butter in a 3-quart saucepan over medium-high heat. When hot, stir to dissolve the sugar and blend in the peanut butter. Bring to a boil. Place the semisweet chocolate in a 3-quart stainless-steel bowl. Pour the boiling cream mixture over the chocolate and allow it to stand for 5 minutes. Stir until smooth.

✳ To assemble the cake, remove the two brownie cakes from the freezer and pour 1 cup of ganache onto each of these layers, using a cake spatula to spread the ganache to the edges. Refrigerate the ganache-covered cake layers for 10 minutes (to allow the ganache to become firm). Remove all of the brownie cake layers from the refrigerator. Stack the 2 ganache-coated layers on top of each other, then top with the uncoated layer and gently press into place. Place the assembled brownie cake layers in the freezer for 10 minutes (lacking freezer space, you may opt to place the cake in the refrigerator for about 30 minutes).

✳ Using a cake spatula, evenly spread ½ cup ganache around the sides of the cake. Pour the remaining ganache onto the top of the cake and use a cake spatula to spread the ganache to the edges. If your kitchen is cool, the ganache may become firm and difficult to pour. If this happens, warm the bowl of ganache over a pan of hot tap water or place the bowl onto a warm heating pad for a minute or two. Use a whisk to gently stir the ganache until smooth.

✳ Press the chopped peanuts onto the ganache on the sides of the cake, coating evenly. Refrigerate the cake for 10 minutes before cutting and serving.

✳ To serve, heat the blade of a serrated slicer under hot running water and wipe the blade dry before cutting each slice. Allow the slices to stand at room temperature for at least 1 hour before serving. The longer the cake is held at room temperature, the gooier the texture will be. The cake may be refrigerated for two to three days after assembly.

NOTE: To prepare peanuts, toast for 10 to 12 minutes in a 325°F oven. Allow the nuts to thoroughly cool before chopping into ⅛-inch pieces.

Smoothest-Ever Truffles

SHIRLEY CORRIHER / REPRINTED FROM *COOKWISE* (WILLIAM MORROW AND COMPANY)

2 cups pecan pieces
7 tablespoons butter
1/4 teaspoon salt
10 to 11 ounces good-quality semisweet chocolate, such as Lindt or Tobler, or 4 bars (2.6 ounces each) Hershey's King Size Special Dark, broken coarsely into 1-inch pieces

6 ounces milk chocolate, broken coarsely into 1-inch pieces
5 large egg yolks
1/4 cup heavy cream
1/4 cup liqueur (Chambord, amaretto, or Grand Marnier)

✱ Preheat the oven to 350°F.

✱ Spread the pecans on a large baking sheet and toast until lightly browned, about 10 to 12 minutes. Remove from the oven and stir in 3 tablespoons of the butter and the salt while the pecans are hot. Let stand until cool to the touch. Chop the pecans in 2 batches in a food processor with the steel knife with quick on/off pulses until finely chopped. Set aside.

✱ Combine the semisweet chocolate and milk chocolate in the food processor with the steel knife and process until finely chopped. Set aside.

✱ Heat the egg yolks and cream in an 8-inch heavy skillet over low heat, stirring constantly with a fork or spatula flat against the bottom of the pan. The split second that you feel thickening, remove the skillet from the heat and keep stirring. Add the remaining 4 tablespoons butter and stir well. Add the chocolate and liqueur. Stir constantly until the chocolate just melts. Continue to stir for 1 minute.

✱ Place the skillet in the refrigerator to set the chocolate. When the chocolate is partly firm, shape the mixture into 1-inch balls with a spoon and roll each in chopped pecans. Keep the truffles covered and refrigerated. Serve in gold fluted candy cups.

MAKES ABOUT THIRTY 1-INCH TRUFFLES

THESE TRUFFLES FEEL LIKE satin IN YOUR MOUTH. CHOPPING THE CHOCOLATE INTO fine PIECES WITH THE FOOD PROCESSOR ensures EVEN MELTING AND USING EGG YOLKS CREATES luxurious SMOOTHNESS.

Old-Fashion Peach Cobbler

SHIRLEY CORRIHER

1 cup orange juice
9 fresh peaches, or 6 cups frozen sliced
  peaches
1 cup granulated sugar
1 tablespoon cornstarch or tapioca starch

1 tablespoon cinnamon
1 tablespoon vanilla extract
4 tablespoons (1/2 stick) butter
1 recipe Simple Flaky Crust (see below)
1/2 gallon good-quality vanilla ice cream

✳ Preheat the oven to 400°F.

✳ Put the orange juice in a large mixing bowl. If using fresh peaches, peel and slice. Place the peach slices in the bowl with the orange juice to prevent discoloration. In a small bowl, stir the sugar, cornstarch, and cinnamon together. Drain the peach slices and add the sugar mixture and vanilla to the bowl; stir well.

✳ Spray a 9 x 13-inch baking dish with nonstick cooking spray. Spoon in the peach mixture. Cut the butter into little chunks and dot throughout the peach mixture.

✳ Roll the crust out to a 9 x 13-inch rectangle and place on top of peaches. Place the baking dish in the oven and bake until the crust is puffed and browned, 30 to 40 minutes.

✳ Serve the cobbler hot or at room temperature with big scoops of vanilla ice cream.

Simple Flaky Crust

SHIRLEY CORRIHER / REPRINTED FROM COOKWISE (WILLIAM MORROW AND COMPANY)

2 cups bleached all-purpose flour
1/2 cup instant flour (Wondra or Shake &
  Blend)
1/2 teaspoon salt

1/2 pound (2 sticks) butter
1 carton (8 ounces) sour cream
1 to 2 tablespoons milk (optional)

✳ In a medium mixing bowl, mix the all-purpose flour, instant flour, and salt. Cut the butter into 1/2-inch cubes, add to the flour mixture, and toss to coat. Place in the freezer for 10 minutes.

✳ Dump the flour-butter mixture on the counter and roll over it with a large rolling pin to flatten the butter lumps. Scrape together and roll over again. Repeat one more time, then scrape back into the bowl and place in the freezer for 5 minutes.

✳ Dump the flour-butter mixture onto the counter and roll and scrape together three more times. Place in the freezer for 10 minutes, then gently fold in the sour cream. The dough should be moist enough to hold together in a ball. Add 1 to 2 tablespoons milk if needed.

✳ Shape the dough into a ball, cover with plastic wrap, and refrigerate for at least 30 minutes before rolling out.

Stars' Sweet Pastry Dough

EMILY LUCHETTI / REPRINTED FROM *STARS' DESSERTS* (HARPERCOLLINS)

2 tablespoons granulated sugar
3 cups flour
1/4 teaspoon salt

12 ounces (3 sticks) cold unsalted butter, cut
  into small pieces
3 tablespoons (approximately) ice cold water

✹ Combine the sugar, flour, and salt in the bowl of an electric mixer. Using the paddle attachment, cut in the butter on low speed until it is the size of small peas.

✹ Slowly pour in just enough water so that the dough just comes together. It should look rough in the bowl but hold together if you squeeze it in your hand.

✹ For pie shells, roll out dough until 1/4 inch thick. For tart shells, roll out dough until 1/8 inch thick. Refrigerate pie or tart shells before baking.

✹ **To prebake a pie or tart shell,** line the pie or tart shell with parchment paper and fill with uncooked rice or dried beans. Bake in a preheated 350°F oven for about 15 minutes, until the edges of the shell are golden brown. Remove the paper and weights. Decrease the temperature to 325°F and continue baking the shell for about 15 minutes, until the bottom of the shell is golden brown.

✹ **To partially bake a pie or tart shell,** bake the tart or pie shell with the parchment paper and the weights until the edges are golden brown, as described above. Remove the parchment paper and weights and bake for 5 minutes more.

✹ If your tart shell cracks on the bottom, make a thick paste out of a little flour and water and seal the crack. Place the tart back in the oven for a few minutes to dry the "glue."

MAKES ONE 9- TO 9¹/₂-INCH TART, OR SIX 4-INCH TARTLETS

HERE IS A RECIPE YOU MAY WANT TO memorize. EMILY'S PASTRY DOUGH IS versatile AND CAN BE USED FOR ANY TYPE OF SWEET PIE, TART, OR TARTLET shell.

 *on Video*

Walnut Crostata

MARCEL DESAULNIERS / REPRINTED FROM *DESSERTS TO DIE FOR* (SIMON & SCHUSTER)

SERVES 8

CROSTATAS ARE TO ITALY WHAT **tarts** ARE TO AMERICA. HOWEVER, **crostatas** BAKE FREE FORM, AND THEIR DOUGH IS ALLOWED TO **expand** WITHOUT BOUNDARIES.

Walnut Crust Dough
1¹/₂ cups all-purpose flour
1 tablespoon granulated sugar, plus
    1 teaspoon
¹/₂ teaspoon salt
¹/₂ cup toasted walnuts, finely chopped
    (see note, page 124)
4 tablespoons (¹/₂ stick) cold unsalted
    butter, cut into 1-tablespoon pieces
2 large egg yolks
3 tablespoons ice water

Cranberry Walnut Filling
1 cup heavy cream
¹/₄ cup granulated sugar
1 cup dried cranberries
1¹/₂ cups toasted walnuts (see note,
    page 124)
¹/₄ teaspoon ground cinnamon

✳ To make the walnut crust dough, place 1¼ cups of the flour, 1 teaspoon sugar, and the salt in the bowl of an electric mixer fitted with a paddle. Mix on low speed for 5 seconds to combine the ingredients. Add all but 2 tablespoons of the chopped walnuts (the reserved walnuts will be sprinkled on the crust just prior to baking) and mix on low speed for 15 seconds. Add the cold butter and mix on low for 1½ to 2 minutes, until the mixture develops a coarse texture. In a small bowl, whisk together 1 of the egg yolks with the ice water. Add the egg-water mixture to the mixing bowl and mix on low for 1 minute, until a loose dough is formed.

✳ Remove the dough from the mixer and form it into a smooth round ball. Wrap the dough in plastic wrap and refrigerate for at least 2 hours. The filling should be prepared as soon as the dough is refrigerated.

✳ To prepare the cranberry walnut filling, heat the heavy cream and sugar in a 3-quart saucepan over medium heat. When hot, stir to dissolve the sugar. Bring to a boil, then adjust the heat and allow to simmer for 6 minutes, until slightly thickened. Remove from the heat and add the cranberries, walnuts, and cinnamon; stir with a rubber spatula to thoroughly combine.

✳ Line a 9-inch pie pan with plastic wrap. Transfer the hot filling to the pie pan, spreading the mixture evenly to the edges. Refrigerate until ready to assemble the crostata.

✳ To assemble and bake the crostata, preheat the oven to 375°F. After the crostata dough has been refrigerated for 2 hours, transfer it to a clean, dry, lightly floured sheet of parchment paper. Roll the dough (using the remaining ¼ cup flour as necessary to prevent the

(continued on next page)

dough from sticking) into a circle about 14 inches in diameter and ⅛ inch thick. Place the rolled dough (leave it on the parchment paper) on a baking sheet. Invert the chilled cranberry and walnut mixture onto the center of the rolled dough (discard the plastic wrap). Fold the edges of the dough towards the center to enclose the cranberry and walnut mixture, leaving a 3½- to 4-inch "window" of fruit and nuts. Refrigerate for 10 minutes.

✱ In a small bowl, whisk the remaining egg yolk. Brush the top of the crostata dough with the whisked yolk. Sprinkle the reserved finely chopped walnuts over the egg-washed dough, then sprinkle with the remaining tablespoon sugar.

✱ Place the baking sheet with the crostata on the center rack of the preheated oven and bake for 30 minutes, until golden brown. Remove the baked crostata from the oven and allow to stand at room temperature for 15 minutes before cutting and serving.

✱ To serve, heat the blade of a serrated knife under hot running water and wipe the blade dry before cutting each slice (as you would a pie or cake).

NOTE: To prepare the walnuts, toast for 12 to 14 minutes in a 325°F oven. Allow the nuts to thoroughly cool before chopping with a food processor or large knife.

Apricot Custard Tart

EMILY LUCHETTI / REPRINTED FROM *4-STAR DESSERTS* (HARPERCOLLINS)

13 ounces (about 5) ripe apricots
One prebaked 9½-inch tart shell (see
   Stars' Sweet Pastry Dough, page 121)
1 cup granulated sugar
2 large egg yolks

¾ cup heavy cream
2 tablespoons all-purpose flour
Pinch of salt
¼ cup (1 ounce) sliced almonds

✱ Preheat the oven to 325°F. Slice the apricots ¾ inch thick, discarding the pits. Place the apricots in the prebaked tart shell in a decorative pattern. Set aside.

✱ Combine the sugar, egg yolks, and cream in a medium mixing bowl. Whisk until combined. Stir in the flour and salt. Carefully pour the creamy mixture over the apricots.

✱ Sprinkle the almonds over the top of the tart. Bake until the custard is almost completely set, about 35 to 40 minutes. Serve slightly warm or at room temperature.

SERVES 6 TO 8

THIS LOVELY SUMMERTIME TART showcases APRICOTS AT THEIR BEST. IT'S ideal TO SERVE AT YOUR NEXT HOT-WEATHER barbecue.

Macaroon Nut Tart

EMILY LUCHETTI / REPRINTED FROM *STARS' DESSERTS* (HARPERCOLLINS)

1 cup sweetened shredded coconut
2¹/₂ ounces unsalted butter
¹/₂ cup firmly packed light brown sugar
4 large egg yolks
1 teaspoon almond extract
¹/₃ cup unsweetened coconut milk

Pinch of salt
3 ounces macadamia nuts, toasted and
   cut in half
1 ounce pecans, toasted
1 partially baked 9-inch tart shell (see
   Stars' Sweet Pastry Dough, page 121)

✳ Preheat the oven to 325°F. Spread the coconut on a baking sheet and toast it for about 10 minutes, until it is light brown.

✳ Increase the oven heat to 350°F. Melt the butter in a small saucepan and stir in the brown sugar.

✳ Put the egg yolks in a large bowl. Stir in the almond extract, coconut milk, and salt. Whisk in the butter mixture. Add the coconut, macadamia nuts, and pecans. Pour the nut filling into the tart shell and smooth the surface with a spatula.

✳ Bake the tart for about 20 minutes, until it is golden brown and just set.

SERVES 6 TO 8

END A TROPICAL-THEMED DINNER WITH THIS COCO-NUT- AND nut-infused TART. SERVE IT WARM FROM THE oven OR COOLED TO ROOM TEMPERATURE.

Caramelized Arequipe Cheesecake

RAFAEL PALOMINO / REPRINTED FROM *BISTRO LATINO* **(WILLIAM MORROW AND COMPANY)**

Two 8-ounce cans sweetened condensed
  milk (do not open)
One 8-ounce package cream cheese, at
  room temperature

6 large eggs
2 cups heavy cream

✱ To caramelize the milk, put the cans in a pot deep enough to hold water to cover the cans, cover with cool water, and bring to a boil over high heat. Once the water has come to a boil, boil the cans for 1 hour and 45 minutes to achieve the best flavor and color, adding more water as needed to keep the cans covered at all times. Never boil the cans for more than two hours: You then run the risk of having them explode. Turn the cans occasionally to stir the milk. Let the cans cool to room temperature before opening.

✱ Preheat the oven to 325°F. In a food processor or electric mixer, process the cream cheese until soft. With the motor running, add the eggs, cream, and caramelized condensed milk. Scrape the mixture into a 9-inch pie dish and place the dish in a roasting pan. Add hot tap water around the dish until it comes halfway up the sides. Bake, uncovered, 60 to 70 minutes. To test for doneness, insert a knife or skewer in the center of the cake—it should come out clean. The top should be dry and golden. Let the cake rest 1 hour to firm up, then serve or refrigerate. If refrigerated, let the cake sit at room temperature for at least 30 minutes before serving.

**MAKES ONE
9-INCH CAKE**

AREQUIPE IS THE NATIONAL DESSERT OF COLOMBIA. IT'S made BY COOKING MILK AND SUGAR UNTIL THICK AND A PALE caramel COLOR. HERE, IT IS GIVEN A new IDENTITY, MASKED IN CHEESECAKE FORM.

Chocolate Cream Puff Ring

SUSAN WESTMORELAND / REPRINTED FROM *THE GOOD HOUSEKEEPING STEP-BY-STEP COOKBOOK* (WILLIAM MORROW AND COMPANY)

Basic Choux Pastry (*see page 132*)

Chocolate Mousse Filling
One 12-ounce package semisweet
   chocolate pieces (2 cups)
1/4 cup milk, plus 1 1/2 teaspoons

3 tablespoons margarine or butter
2 large eggs
2 cups heavy cream

1 1/2 teaspoons light corn syrup
1 pint strawberries (optional)

✱ Preheat the oven to 400°F. Lightly grease and flour a cookie sheet. Using a 7-inch plate as a guide, trace a circle in flour on the cookie sheet. Prepare the basic choux pastry.

✱ Drop the choux pastry batter by heaping tablespoons into 12 mounds, inside circle, to form a ring. With a moistened finger, smooth the tops. Bake for 40 minutes, or until golden. Turn off the oven; let the ring stand in the oven 15 minutes. Remove the ring from the oven; cool on the cookie sheet or a wire rack.

✱ Meanwhile, prepare the chocolate mousse filling: In a heavy 3-quart saucepan, heat 1 1/2 cups of the semisweet chocolate pieces (reserve remaining 1/2 cup for glaze), 1/4 cup milk (reserve the remaining 1 1/2 teaspoons for the glaze), and 2 tablespoons of the margarine (reserve the remaining 1 tablespoon for the glaze) over low heat, stirring occasionally, until smooth. Add the eggs, one at a time, stirring constantly with a wire whisk. Cool.

✱ In a large bowl, with a mixer at medium speed, beat the cream until stiff peaks form. With a rubber spatula, fold the whipped cream into the cooled chocolate mixture, half at a time, until blended.

✱ With a long serrated knife, cut the cooled ring horizontally in half. Spoon the chocolate mousse filling into the bottom of the ring. Replace the top of the ring. Refrigerate until ready to serve.

✱ In a heavy 1-quart saucepan, heat the reserved 1/2 cup semisweet chocolate pieces, the remaining 1 tablespoon margarine, 1 1/2 teaspoons milk, and the light corn syrup over low heat, stirring occasionally, until smooth. Spoon the glaze over the ring. Fill the center of the ring with strawberries, if desired.

(continued on next page)

SERVES 12

A basic BATTER, MADE ON THE STOVETOP, IS THE FOUNDATION FOR A PUFFY pastry RING. FILL IT ACCORDING TO YOUR WHIM, WITH CHOCOLATE MOUSSE, WHIPPED CREAM, STRAWBERRIES, OR A LITTLE OF EACH. A drizzle OF SEMISWEET CHOCOLATE GLAZE TOPS IT OFF NICELY.

Basic Choux Pastry

¹/₂ cup (1 stick) margarine or butter
¹/₄ teaspoon salt
1 cup water

1 cup all-purpose flour
4 large eggs

✳ In a 3-quart saucepan, heat the margarine, salt, and water over medium heat until the margarine melts and the mixture boils. Remove from heat. With a wooden spoon, vigorously stir in the flour all at once until the mixture forms a ball and leaves the side of pan.

✳ Add the eggs to the flour mixture, one at a time, beating well after each addition, until the mixture is smooth and satiny. Shape and bake the warm batter as directed.

Lazy Daisy Cake

MARION CUNNINGHAM / REPRINTED FROM *THE FANNY FARMER COOKBOOK* **(RANDOM HOUSE)**

2 eggs
1 teaspoon vanilla extract
1 cup granulated sugar
1 cup flour
1 teaspoon baking powder
¹/₄ teaspoon salt

¹/₂ cup milk
4 tablespoons (¹/₂ stick) butter
3 tablespoons dark brown sugar
2 tablespoons heavy cream
¹/₂ cup grated coconut or chopped nuts

✳ Preheat the oven to 350°F. Butter and lightly flour an 8-inch square cake pan.

✳ In a large mixing bowl, beat the eggs with the vanilla until they have thickened slightly. Gradually add the granulated sugar and beat thoroughly.

✳ Mix the flour, baking powder, and salt together and add to the first mixture, blending until smooth.

✳ Heat the milk and 1 tablespoon of the butter together in a small pan. When the butter has melted, quickly stir the milk and melted butter into the batter and mix well; the batter will be very liquid. Quickly pour the batter into the pan and bake for about 25 minutes, until a toothpick comes out clean. Remove the cake from the oven.

✳ Mix the remaining 3 tablespoons butter, the brown sugar, cream, and coconut or nuts together in a small pan over low heat until melted and well blended. Spread over the hot cake and brown lightly under the broiler for a minute or two, taking care that it does not burn.

MAKES ONE 8-INCH SQUARE CAKE

A 1950'S AFTER-SCHOOL treat HAS SURVIVED THE TEST OF TIME. BROILED COCONUT, BROWN SUGAR, AND CHOPPED NUTS ARE THIS CAKE'S signature topping.

PERMISSIONS

From *4-Star Desserts* by Emily Luchetti (HarperCollins, 1996) ©1996 by Emily Luchetti: Apricot Custard Tart, Warm Bittersweet Chocolate Tartlets with Spiced Almonds, Spiced Almonds

From *Bistro Latino* by Rafael Palomino (William Morrow & Company, 1998) ©1998 by Rafael Palomino: Caramelized Arequipe Cheesecake, Garlic Shrimp and Pineapple Skewers, Grilled Steak Marinated in Citrus, New World Paella, Potato-Chipotle Gratin

From *Chilis to Chutneys: American Home Cooking with the Flavors of India* by Neelam Batra (William Morrow & Company, 1998) ©1998 by Neelam Batra: Chicken Tandoori, Chicken Tikka Masala, Tandoori Chicken Salad with Ginger-Mint Dressing, Ginger-Mint Dressing

From *Cooking to Beat the Clock* by Sam Gugino, et al. (Chronicle Books, 1999) ©1999 by Sam Gugino, et al.: Chicken Fajitas with Mango Salsa, Fifteen-Minute Bouillabaisse

From *CookWise* by Shirley Corriher (William Morrow & Company, 1997) ©1997 by Shirley Corriher: All-Time Favorite Sour Cream Cornbread, Best-Ever Marinated Shrimp, Cheddar-Crusted Chicken Breasts with Grapes and Apples in Grand Marnier Sauce, Parmesan-Crusted Zucchini Fans, Salmon Fillet with Sweet, Grainy Mustard Crust, Sherried Rice and Barley with Almonds, Simple Flaky Crust, Smoothest-Ever Truffles

From *Death by Chocolate Cookies* by Marcel Desaulniers (Simon & Schuster, 1997) ©1997 by Marcel Desaulniers: Chocolate Cashew Coconut Clusters

From *Desserts to Die For* by Marcel Desaulniers (Simon & Schuster, 1995) ©1995 by Marcel Desaulniers: Gooey Chocolate Peanut Butter Brownie Cake, Walnut Crostata

From *Entertaining Light and Easy* by Laurie Burrows Grad (Simon & Schuster, 1998) ©1998 by Laurie Burrows Grad: Gratin of Yukon Gold Potatoes, Instant Strawberry-Peach Frozen Yogurt, Rack of Lamb with Pistachio-Mint Crumb Crust and Tangy Mint Sauce, Sun-Dried Tomato and Basil Chicken Paté

From *Fast and Festive Meals for the Jewish Holidays* by Marlene Sorosky, et al. (William Morrow & Company, 1997) ©1997 by Marlene Sorosky, et al.: Brisket with Burgundy-Orange Sauce, Chocolate Cherry Dreidel Cake, Crisp Potato Kugel, Crowned Apple Cake, Giant Potato-Carrot Pancake, Lamb Shanks with Portobello Mushrooms and Dried Cranberries, Matzah Balls

From *Good Housekeeping Step-by-Step Cookbook* by the editors of *Good Housekeeping Magazine* (William Morrow and Company, 1997) ©1997 by *Good Housekeeping Magazine*: Basic Choux Pastry, Chocolate Cream-Puff Ring, Golden Onion Focaccia, Harvest Casserole, Roast Beef Tenderloin, Zucchini Ribbons with Mint

From *Incredible Cuisine* by Jean Pierre Brehier (Time-Life Books, 1997) ©1997 by Jean Pierre Brehier: Butternut Squash & Bourbon Bisque, Chicken Breasts Stuffed with Herb Cream Cheese & Smoked Ham on a Bed of Arugula, Coq au Vin, Mustard & Balsamic Vinaigrette, Herb Cream Cheese

From *Italy al Dente* by Biba Caggiano (William Morrow & Company, 1998) ©1998 by Biba Caggiano: Pasta and Bean Soup Neapolitan Style, Risotto with Roasted Red Bell Peppers, Spaghetti with Fried Bread Crumbs, Pancetta and Hot Pepper

From *John Willingham's World Champion Bar-B-Q* by John Willingham (William Morrow & Company, 1996) ©1996 by John Willingham: Sweet 'n Sassy Beans, Sweet Bar-B-Q Sauce, Willingham's World Champion Ribs, Mild Seasoning Mix

From *Learning to Cook with Marion Cunningham* by Marion Cunningham (Knopf, 1999) ©1999 by Marion Cunningham: James Beard's Roasted Spareribs, Polenta Baked with Vegetables

From *License to Grill by Chris Schlesinger*, et al. (William Morrow & Company, 1997) ©1997 by Chris Schlesinger, et al.: Chipotle-Rubbed Grilled Skirt Steak with Grill-Roasted Bananas, Grilled Apple and Bread Salad with Arugula, Blue Cheese, and Grapes, Grilled Regular Mushrooms with Sherry, Smoky Ratatouille for a Crowd,

From *Lobster at Home* by Jasper White (Scribner, 1998) ©1998 by Jasper White: Traditional Lobster Salad, The World-Famous Maine Lobster Roll, Baked Stuffed Lobster

From *Saveur Cooks Authentic American*, by the editors of *Saveur Magazine* (Chronicle Books, 1998) ©1998 by *Saveur Magazine*: Creamed Spinach, French Fries, Gus's Fried Chicken

From *Seasons Greetings: Cooking and Entertaining for Thanksgiving, Christmas, and New Year's* by Marlene Sorosky (Chronicle Books, 1997) ©1997 by Marlene Sorosky: Crab-Stuffed Mushrooms, Mini Corn Muffins with Chilies and Cheese, Maple-Glazed Roast Pork with Maple-Mustard Sauce, Zucchini Sausage Squares

From *Stars' Desserts* by Emily Luchetti (Harper Collins, 1991) ©1991 by Emily Luchetti: Macaroon Nut Tart, Stars' Sweet Pastry Dough

From *The Fanny Farmer Cookbook* by Marion Cunningham (Random House, 1996) ©1996 by Marion Cunningham: Lazy Daisy Cake

From *The Good Housekeeping Illustrated Children's Cookbook* by the editors of *Good Housekeeping Magazine* (William Morrow & Company, 1997) ©1997 *Good Housekeeping Magazine*: Pizza

From *The Magic Spoon Cookbook* by Suzanne Gooding (Klutz Press, 1997) ©1997 by Suzanne Gooding: Designer Pretzels, Spicy Chicken Little Drumsticks

From *The New Elegant But Easy Cookbook* by Marian Burros, et al. (Simon & Schuster, 1998) ©1998 by Marian Burros, et al.: Baked Imperial Chicken, Cumberland Sauce, Lemon Angel Trifle, Macaroni and Cheese, the Canal House, Toasted Mushroom Rolls

From *The Pie and Pastry Bible* by Rose Levy Beranbaum (Charles Scribner's Sons, 1998) ©1998 by Rose Levy Beranbaum: Brownie Puddle

From *The Splendid Table* by Lynne Rossetto Kasper (William Morrow & Company, 1992) ©1992 by Lynne Kasper: Baked Maccheroni with Winter Tomato Sauce, Winter Tomato Sauce, Christmas Capon, Garganelli with Roasted Peppers, Peas, and Cream, Tagliatelle with Caramelized Oranges and Almonds

From *The Trellis Cookbook* by Marcel Desaulniers (Fireside, 1992) ©1992 by Marcel Desaulniers: Curried Apple and Onion Soup, Grilled Medallions of Pork with Sweet Potatoes, Cranberries, and Pine Nuts

From *The Wisdom of the Chinese Kitchen* by Grace Young (Simon & Schuster, 1999) ©1999 by Grace Young: Barbecued Pork, Fried Rice, Tender Chicken on Rice, Tomato Beef

The following recipes are courtesy of

Shirley Corriher:
Old-Fashion Peach Cobbler

Robert Clark:
Bacon-Wrapped Scallops with Potato-Mushroom Cake

Denis Blais:
Twice-Baked Brie and Roasted Pepper Soufflés with Olive Tapenade, Grilled Lamb Loin with Eggplant and Spiced Couscous Rolls

Chris Johnson:
Chili Salmon Spring Rolls with Oyster Sauce, Grilled Pork Loin with Apple and Zucchini

---

Home Cooking with Amy Coleman © 1999 by Marjorie Poore Productions
Photography by Darla Furlani

Design: Kari Perin, Perin + Perin
Project Management and Editing: Jennifer L. Newens
Editing: Carol M. Newman
Production: Kristen Wurz

ISBN 0-9651095-3-4
Printed in Hong Kong through Global Interprint

10 9 8 7 6 5 4 3 2 1

MPP Books
363 14th Avenue, San Francisco, CA 94118
Distributed by Bristol Publishing Enterprises, Inc.

The **KitchenAid** Story

A HUMBLE BEGINNING *The modern KitchenAid stand mixer began with a single drop of sweat off the end of a busy baker's nose. The year was 1908, and Herbert Johnston, an engineer and later president of the Hobart Manufacturing Company in Troy, Ohio, was watching the baker mix bread dough with an age-old iron spoon. To help ease that burden, Johnston pioneered the development of an eighty-quart mixer. By 1915 professional bakers had an easier, more thorough, and more sanitary way of mixing their wares.*

In fact, that amazing, labor-saving machine caught on so quickly that the United States Navy ordered Hobart mixers for its three new battleships —The California, The Tennessee, *and* The South Carolina. *By 1917 the mixer was classified as "regular equipment" on all U.S. Navy ships.*

The success of the commercial mixer gave Hobart engineers inspiration to create a mixer suitable for the home. But World War I interfered, and the concept of a home mixer was put on hold.

1919

THE BIRTH OF A KITCHEN ICON

1919 was truly a time of change. The gray days of war were giving way to the gaiety of the Roaring Twenties. The spark of women's suffrage had ignited and women across America would soon earn the right to vote. America was on the brink of an era of peace and prosperity, and progress was the cry from the factory to the farm.

War munitions plants across the country were busily converting to peace-time production. Meanwhile, a small manufacturing company in a sleepy, southwest Ohio town revived its effort to design the first electrical "food preparer" for the home.

And so it did! The first home stand mixer was born in 1919 at the Troy Metal Products Company, a subsidiary of the Hobart Manufacturing Company. The progeny of the large commercial food mixers, the Model H-5 was the first in a long line of quality home food preparers that utilized "planetary action." Planetary action was a revolutionary design that rotated the beater in one direction while moving it around the bowl in the opposite direction.

The wives of Troy executives tested the initial prototypes. While discussing possible names for the new machine, one homemaker commented, "I don't care what you call it, but I know it's the best kitchen aid I have ever had!" Hence, a brand name was born, and the first KitchenAid stand mixer was unveiled to the American consumer.

> ## "I don't care what you call it, but I know it's the best kitchen aid I have ever had!"

The KitchenAid H-5 rolled off the newly founded KitchenAid Manufacturing Company's assembly line at the rate of four per day and was priced at $189.50. The overriding concern then, as now, was that every KitchenAid produced would be of unsurpassed quality. Nothing would be shipped to customers that was not tested and retested.

But retail dealers were reluctant to undertake the selling of the unique "food preparer." So KitchenAid set out to sell its stand mixers door-to-door with a largely female sales force (strong enough to carry the 65-lb. Model H-5 on sales calls). Homemakers were encouraged to invite friends to their homes, where the KitchenAid salesperson would prepare food for the group showcasing the new stand mixer. By the 1930s the KitchenAid had earned wide acceptance, and dealers began to show interest.

1920–1930s

MEETING THE CONSUMERS' NEEDS

In the mid-1920s production had increased to five mixers per day, which was considered excellent efficiency by the standards of the day. Prices had declined to $150 (approximately $1,500 in today's dollars), and the company offered an easy payment program of 10% down and 10% per month for 10 months with no interest.

By the late 1920s American kitchens were growing smaller. KitchenAid responded with a smaller, lighter stand mixer at a lower price. The Model G proved so popular that the Model H-5 was stopped.

1930s

The 1930s brought the Depression, and with it, rising unemployment. The model G was beyond the financial means of most Americans, so KitchenAid confronted the problem. Within three years KitchenAid introduced three new models that were less expensive and within the means of many American households.

In the midst of the great dust bowl years, social upheaval, and joblessness, KitchenAid planners laid a solid foundation that would support the stand mixer's growth for the next six decades. KitchenAid recruited Egmont Arens, a nationally acclaimed editor and world-renowned designer, to design three new stand mixer models. Arens's designs were so timelessly simple and functional that they remain virtually unchanged to this day.

1937

THE MODEL K

The Model K, first introduced in 1937, was more compact, moderately priced ($55), and capable of powering all the attachments. Every model introduced since has allowed for fully interchangeable attachments—a tribute to common sense and management of resources.

By the late 1930s, demand for KitchenAid stand mixers was so great that the factory could not keep up and sold out before Christmas each year. But in 1941 World War II intervened and the plant focused its production on munitions. During the war years there was limited production of KitchenAid stand mixers.

...the name KitchenAid has become synonymous with quality to generations of Americans.

As peace arrived and the troops came home, production of the KitchenAid stand mixer began again in earnest. KitchenAid moved to Greenville, Ohio, to expand the production. Greenville, is still the home of the factory where the dedicated employees of that community have proudly produced the stand mixer, and now other KitchenAid products, for more than half a century.

1950–1997
SEEN IN ALL THE BEST PLACES

KitchenAid, always in the forefront of trends, introduced daring new colors at the 1955 Atlantic City Housewares Show. The new colors—Petal Pink, Sunny Yellow, Island Green, Satin Chrome, and Antique Copper—were a bold departure from the white appliances seen in most kitchens of the time. To this day KitchenAid offers the standard classics, along with a variety of decorative colors.

Today, the legacy of quality lives on not only in the multifunctional stand mixer, but also in a full line of kitchen appliances sold across the world. Every product that carries the KitchenAid name, whether purchased in Paris or Peoria, is guaranteed to be strong, reliable and versatile—each backed by over 75 years of quality and excellence.

The distinctive silhouette of KitchenAid appliances can be seen in some of America's most famous home and restaurant kitchens. "Home Cooking" with Amy Coleman—which KitchenAid is proud to sponsor as part of an ongoing commitment to nurturing the talents of home chefs—marks the latest of many cooking shows that have relied on KitchenAid appliances to perform faultlessly and enhance the decor of their sets. Viewers of "Friends," "Cybill," and other television shows will see the appliances prominently displayed, and even used on occasion, in these sitcom kitchens. And finding a top restaurant without at least one hard-working KitchenAid stand mixer would be a real challenge.

Even museums, the ultimate showcases for design excellence, feature KitchenAid products on display. San Francisco's avant-garde Museum of Modern Art, for example, featured the KitchenAid stand mixer in an exhibit of American icons. There is even a KitchenAid stand mixer in the esteemed collection of the Smithsonian Institution.

From humble beginnings among the cornfields of southwest Ohio, the name KitchenAid has become synonymous with quality. Although over the years KitchenAid has streamlined and updated its stand mixer design and technology, the worldwide success of KitchenAid can be traced to the solid foundation set back in 1919.